The Independent Consultant's Survival Guide

Starting up and succeeding as a self-employed consultant

Mike Johnson

cipd

Chartered Institute of Personnel and Development

Published by the Chartered Institute of Personnel and Development
151 The Broadway, London SW19 1JQ

First published 2005
© Chartered Institute of Personnel and Development, 2005

Typeset by Ferdinand Page Design, Surrey
Printed in Great Britain by The Cromwell Press, Trowbridge, Wiltshire

British Library Cataloguing in Publication Data
A catalogue of this manual is available from the British Library

ISBN 1-84398-116-5

Chartered Institute of Personnel and Development,
151 The Broadway, London, SW19 1JQ
Tel: 020 8612 6200
E-mail: cipd@cipd.co.uk Website: www.cipd.co.uk
Incorporated by Royal Charter. Registered Charity No. 1079797

Contents

Acknowledgements

As always, there are lots of people who 'influence' a book. I suppose in this case it is the hundreds – probably thousands – of independents I have met over the years. However, I would like to thank particularly some of the 'usual suspects' whose opinion I always seem to be asking for: must mean I think they are pretty smart! To save them from arguing about who has had the most influence on me, I have placed them in alphabetical order.

Thanks to Rai Barbour, a towering artistic talent, who carved a second, great independent career in his 70s; Cliff Dennett, for showing me how the new generation is going to do it; Mike Devlin, for thousands of ideas – trust your sell-out to 'big' business doesn't last too long; Hanneke Frese, for all your help – and welcome to the 'real' world after those years in the wilderness; Labeed Hamid, for 30 years of free advice, and I still need it; Neil Irons – the very epitome of the lone consultant, and his staff think so too! His advice is priceless (which is why I never paid him); Shay McConnon, consultant *extraordinaire*, magician and friend. Pulls rabbits out of hats for his clients and cabaret audiences; Darryl Narey, painter-decorator, and a man who knows more about client relationships than anyone I have ever met; Richard Savage, a corporate suit turned good guy, who regularly helps the needy (me!); Susan Stucky, a shrewd West Coast observer of the profession, who has forgotten more than I will ever learn; and Nick Winkfield, a much used, abused and appreciated 'shoulder to cry on', usually after bottle number two!

And also to Khalid Aziz, Tony Buzan, Anne Chivers, Rene Cordeiro, Vincent Dominé, Richard Donkin, Christian Goffin, Rosie Halfhead, Pam Hurley, Isabel Hutchings, John Jeffcock, Vera Lenaerts, Dave Lovett, Jens Maier, Trevor Marsden, Janice Nagourney, Wim Noortman, Peppi Seppal, Catie Thorburn, Tamas Toth, Alper Utku, Laurence VanHee and Norman Walker for their wise advice, counsel and input to the book. Yes, I was listening to you!

Very special thanks to my accountant Peter Clegg of Westlake Clark for agreeing to be my expert on the numbers, and the co-author of Chapter 6.

Thanks to Stephen Partridge, commissioning editor at the CIPD, for the idea for the book and his support in getting it into production.

Finally, thanks to my old friend John Humble, doyen of the independent consultants, who first suggested that I escape corporate life and go out and 'do something useful'. Well, I tried!

Mike Johnson

Foreword

Chances are that if you've picked up this book you are at the very least thinking about taking that big step and GOING IT ALONE. Well, you've come to the right place. This book is about both getting you ready to be a successful independent consultant and, once you're set, developing your business and staying the course.

The concept of *The Independent Consultant's Survival Guide* is simple. It is a practical, how-to guide to becoming a working professional consultant. All the other books on this subject I have looked at seem to be not books at all, but lists of things to do. Well, there are lists of things to do in here as well: but I think the most helpful parts are the anecdotes about what I – and others – have experienced in running our own small firms.

What I have tried to do is give you an idea of some of the challenges you will face and some of the methods to deal with them. The book breaks down into three parts:

- getting set to go on your own
- how to survive once you are an independent
- an in-depth look at the financial and legal implications and obligations.

Working for yourself – whatever your specialisation – isn't easy. It takes courage, hard work and, most probably, some luck too; but more than that, it takes ENTHUSIASM, and the will to succeed. I started my independent consulting career in 1982 and have been lucky in the fact that I have enjoyed 90 per cent of that time (I bet few people toiling in the corporate world of big business can say that).

And I use the term 'independent consultant' in its very broadest sense. Whether you are a working mother, a bored employee, a young graduate or even a would-be tree surgeon, this book is aimed directly at YOU. I don't care what you call yourself, I don't care how you dress or what your expertise is. This book is designed to give you the basics to get going and to be a success. In fact, it is really a guide for anyone who is thinking of going it alone – from architects to plumbers, accountants to electricians, all are welcome.

I hope you enjoy the book and, more than that, I hope it persuades you to join our exciting and fulfilling profession.

Mike Johnson
Little Buckland Farm
Hollywood Lane
Lymington
Hampshire SO41 9HD
United Kingdom
mikeajohnson@compuserve.com
www.mikeajohnson.com

Introduction

As I said in the Foreword, if you are not going to go into this with enthusiasm don't go into it at all. Enthusiasm will get you through most things. If you are just doing it for the money, it probably won't work.

There is a key reason for this introduction – and it can save you money. All I want you to do is quickly work through the short test on the next page. If you score under 60, put the book back and go out and seek a different career path.

Be as honest as you can in answering. We get into more detailed questions later in the book, but this Introduction will tell you three critical things about working for yourself:

- Have I the temperament to do it?
- Have I the contacts and support that I will need to survive?
- Do I have the right skill sets to be successful in the long term?

If you don't match up to this, there really is a risk that you will fail. Countless people try to go it alone and don't make it. They may struggle for a few months or even a few years, but in the end one of those three legs of success above collapses under the pressure.

THE GET UP AND GO-IT-ALONE QUIZ [1]

Write in a number between 1 (low) and 10 (high) about how this question applies to you – **BE HONEST!**

	Score: 1–10
Temperament	
– Self-motivated, able to multi-task	...
– Willingness to study and learn	...
– Perseverance	...
– Tolerance of uncertainty and risk	...
Support	
– Good business and professional networks	...
– Reliable personal/family support system	...
– Physical and mental energy	...
– Enough in the bank to 'survive' for six months	...
Skills	
– Communication skills	...
– Time management skills	...
– Transportable professional skills and knowledge	...
– Skills that will not be obsolete in a couple of years	...
Total score	...

[1] Adapted from a concept by Nick Winkfield of Stakeholder Studies www.stakeholderstudies.com

On the basis of your total score, this is what action you should take now.

Under 60: stay in your job, or find a new one, but don't try and work for yourself

60–90: think twice (develop those skill sets you will need)

Over 90: do it now!

Of course, there are lots of other criteria to base a decision on, but the 12 used in this quiz will give you a quick guide to whether you have the personality, effective support and the required skills to make a go of it.

If you did score more than 90, then let's move on and begin to outline all the steps you are going to have to take to make sure that you succeed. We start in Chapter One, with a very basic question that most people never ask themselves: why do you want to do it?

Chapter 1

Think about it – then think some more

What the hell do you want to work for somebody else for? Work for yourself!

Irving Berlin to *George Gershwin*

Belief in magic did not disappear when our ancestors stopped painting themselves blue. The more difficult the problems we face the more we yearn for the outsider with the magic wand. Corporate leaders have come to rely on the latter-day counterpart of the magician: the consultant.

John J. Tarrant, Drucker, the Man Who Invented the Corporate Society

Why do you want to do it?

If you haven't really thought through why you want to become an independent consultant, we can end the book right here. For the simple answer to anyone who hasn't taken the trouble to really examine their reasons is – DON'T DO IT!

In the 20-plus years that I have been working as an independent consultant, I have witnessed all sorts of reasons for wanting to 'hang up your shingle at the door' (as the Americans say), and to feel that wondrous tingle of freedom, just before that *frisson* of fear shoots down your backbone. And let me tell you, a little fear is a good thing indeed. Or to put it more plainly still, if you can't muster up a good helping of paranoia when required, you'll never make it as an independent anything.

As I have already pointed out in the Foreword, this book is about the practicalities of embarking on life as a stand-alone consultant. Sure you may have a partner, you may have a network: but believe me, you *are* on your own. Only you can make a success of this foray into a new kind of business. So from the outset you need to know, deep down inside, why you want to do this.

None of the following is a good basis for going it alone:

- You have a fight with your boss and resolve never to work there again.
- You fail to get a promotion in the organisation and think you can do better on the outside.
- You are made redundant, fired or similar and think it is an easy option to earn some money until another job comes along.
- You go on holiday and decide you want to live in a French/Italian/ Spanish/Greek hamlet and raise pigs/wine/olives (please delete as appropriate). Although, joking apart, 'planned' downshifting is a huge trend, which is certainly going to continue.

Discord, disappointment, desperation and daydreaming are not good reasons: like all things that are ultimately successful, trying to go it alone takes planning and, most of all, enthusiasm and commitment to the idea.

Be a lion tamer, it's safer

Depending on what table of statistics you read, working for yourself is a very dangerous occupation that makes test pilots, mercenaries and lion tamers look like sensible people. Why? Well, two-thirds of test pilots, mercenaries and lion tamers don't fail in the first two years – two-thirds of independents do. This makes anyone's transition to independent status fraught with risk. But go back and carry out post-mortems with those who didn't make it (which, while we are handing out advice, is a great idea) and you'll find that – swingeing bad luck apart – you can put 90 per cent of that failure down to either a complete lack of preparation, or a simple naïve belief that it was going to be easy.

Let's get something straight from the outset: it isn't easy. If it were easy, everyone would do it. If it were easy, two-thirds wouldn't go down with their ship in the first 730 days. Oh, and that's how long you've got if you work all the hours, days and weeks God sends. If you take weekends off and play golf on Wednesdays, you've only got 468 days to succeed.

Given the odds against success and the time commitment you have to put in to have any chance of making it, you can't help but wonder if the people who take this route to an independent career are in any way sane. My view – and this is personal and has no bearing in scientific fact whatever – is that most successful independents are mad (in a nice way of course). If they weren't, I don't think that many could put up with the high and lows, successes and failures that are the typical topography of any independent's existence.

Independence, the new, new thing

Of course, as well-meaning friends and givers of advice, we can spend hours – usually in bars or around kitchen tables on rainy Sunday afternoons – debating the pros and cons of putting that great idea into action, or taking your hard-earned knowledge and going it alone. We can tell our best friends that they are 'insane' (see above), 'totally wrong mentally', 'too lazy', 'too broke' or 'too impatient' ever to contemplate going it alone. Most of these friends won't ever do it, for the reasons we outlined above. But increasingly in this early part of the twenty-first century, more and more will.

As became clearly evident in the research for an earlier book,[1] there is a growing feeling – especially among working professionals in the 20–35 age group in most countries – that there has got to be something better than the one-hour commute and working for some large corporation. You can work for MegaCorp for a while (at least until you soak up all the knowledge they can give you, and you build a stake in society), but after that it is time to look at some alternatives.

But this isn't confined to the young – people in their fifties and sixties (who have zero debt) are redefining their lifestyles and downshifting. More often than not, this includes some kind of plan for independent work: and independent consultants represent a huge majority of these people. As we shall see later on, technology has allowed all of us to work remotely more than ever before.[2]

Indeed, major employers in Europe and the USA are slowly beginning to realise that such is the drift away from mainstream employment that these wannabe independent consultants are going to be a key component of their employment mix. Outsourcing isn't confined to India and China: it is equally at home wherever these professional downshifters have chosen to put down roots. This might not be in some exotic locale, or in the countryside – many people continue to live in the same town or city, and just redefine what they want to achieve in a different way. The crisis for big corporations is that without these highly trained professionals, they will face a long-term lack of talent. And while this isn't the key role of this book, it is important to keep in mind that as more and more people desire to downshift and take the independent consultant option there will be more and more infrastructure to support this new career choice.

[1] Johnson, M. (2004) *The New Rules of Engagement: Life-work balance and employee commitment.* London: CIPD.

[2] Datamonitor estimates 12 million downshifters in Europe.

So, while there have always been a few independent spirits about, we are now really seeing a mass explosion in the number of people lining up to take the 'indie challenge.'

Have you got a plan?

The first step on the road to an independent future comes at a price. You have to sit down – preferably with someone you trust to tell you the truth – and really work out what you want to do, how you are going to do it, and where the support to achieve it is going to come from. It is all about assessing yourself – *very* honestly indeed. Before we get into some of the detail below, here are a few scenarios to get you thinking:

- You are young; you are single; you have zero savings; you have a great idea, and you want to quit the job you hate to make it work. The hard truth is that unless you have rich parents or relations who believe in you and can give you a no-strings-attached loan, you are going nowhere. Without security, no bank is going to lend you the money at anything like a rate you can repay. Advice: work hard at the job you have and save a stake to start on your great idea when you can.

  Tip! When you have a big enough financial stake to live for six months with no income, that's the time to try.

- You are living with a partner; you have two children who are both at school; you have a house loan about the size of the national debt of Albania; you want to start working for yourself. Advice: if your employer will give you are guaranteed contract for, say, two years that will cover your basic outgoings, then consider it. Otherwise wait until someone – or several clients – will give you that basic guarantee. You need to be solvent and able to see an income stream.
- You are 55; you and your spouse have waved goodbye to the children; you own your house; you've always wanted to open your own boutique consulting firm. Advice: again, try and do a deal with your employer, or volunteer for early retirement. If you need to, downshift your house and release start-up capital. All the same, ideally don't go and burn capital, look for an income solution.

Seven, five or three days a week

In the past, independent consultants have fallen into three distinct categories: the younger professional who wants to try out his or her own ideas and gain a broader experience; the mature professional who feels he or she can get more variety acting on his or her own; and the super-specialist who is hired for his or her unique expertise. These people, with few exceptions, worked a full working week, and often into the weekend. The exact amount of work they did probably depended on business cycles and seasons. For example, at certain times of the year, independent accountants would have found themselves working all hours to meet the deadlines for their clients' filing with tax authorities. Others, like management development specialists, would have had busy periods that coincided with key points in their clients' year. However, the fact remained that if you weren't 'working', you were 'looking for work'.

Today, however, this concept has been firmly hit on the head. What we are now seeing – driven in particular by this rash of newcomers to the Indie brigade – are many new consultants who have very specific ideas about how long, how hard, where, why and when they will work. So, for example, I know an international tax specialist who works two days a week on average (charging large fees, I should add), but spends four other days a week in competitive sailing. He now charges for both (he runs sailing courses where most of his wealthy customers are his tax clients too!). Equally, I have a long-time friend who runs a horse ranch in the USA (his dream finally realised), but acts as the senior management development executive for his former company. These people are just as much independent consultants as a newly qualified accountant or people development specialist who decides he wants to build his own practice. The only difference is that they are at different stages of their life, with different wants, needs and expectations.

Similarities count most

It isn't the differences that are important, it is the SIMILARITIES that count when looking at what makes a successful independent consultant. Not clear about the similarities? Not too sure how a two days a week, yacht-racing, international tax adviser is similar to a just qualified accountant? Well, there are three things that make them the same – and successful:

- They are focused: they know exactly what they want and have gone out to get it.
- They have a plan and they live with it and for it.
- They are flexible and equipped for change.

Consultant, know thyself

What I am going to show you – and to stress – throughout this book is that successful independent consultants might appear different from each other. They might be in different professions, from different backgrounds, with different lifestyles, and at different stages in their careers. But if you look under the surface, there are a lot more similarities than differences.

My tax consultant friend knows that five or six times each year he'll have to pull a late night or two. Possibly head off to some West Indian island or whatever (where the sailing is equally good!) to keep up his reputation, standards and the confidence of the clients. However, the key to his success is that he knows what he wants and how to organise for that – totally. Do not equate success to hours worked or even income earned. Today, for the independent consultant it is not about that. It is about what you have decided works best for you. And that includes knowing when you will have to move just a little out of your own personal 'envelope' to achieve it.

I have another friend, a hugely successful motivational consultant. For years I was under the assumption that he worked non-stop. Every time I was at a conference, he was there too. Every time I had a meeting with him the phone rang constantly, and he was taking 'orders' for his time. It wasn't until I got to know him really well that I discovered he actually works three weeks on and two weeks off. He has done this for the last 10 years and no one else knows. The reason no one else knows is that he never tells them. They call him and say, 'Can you come in on Tuesday next?' The reply goes like this: 'Sorry, I'd love to, but I'm travelling all week.' He never, *ever* says, 'Well, I'll be on holiday.' So he never really lets them down and they think he is hugely busy, which enhances his reputation and puts him more in demand rather than less. His view is that he is prepared to give up work to meet his lifestyle needs. He wouldn't have done that early in his career, but now he can afford to (in Chapter 2 we tackle the great vacation dilemma and how to overcome it).

Tip! You must set rules for yourself from the outset – it is a difficult discipline to master, but it needs to be done.

So as we get into the depths of this book, let us not forget that you do things for the client, but you must set rules for yourself too. Fail to do that and you will never be successful. There are times when you just have to say, 'No, I can't do that right now.' And then you have to understand the hardest truth of all: despite whatever else you have done for them in the past, when you've said no, the client may well not come back. They'll find someone else. So you have to become like my friend, and be travelling next week. Get them used to that. Play by your rules not theirs.

Now I concede that this may be a difficult idea to swallow if you are about to embark on a solo career. And I also concede that you may well run yourself ragged in those early years in order to get a foot on the ladder of success. But, in so doing, the thing you need to ask yourself is, 'Will any of my clients really respect me?' In my view, and in my experience, they won't. What you need to do is set limits. How you deal with and react to a client in the early days sets the pattern for your relationship (more about that later). But if you want to be happy, not to mention successful and valued, the words are 'Consultant, know thyself', and know what you will and will not do.

This applies to all of us. Of course, there is a tendency to look at the outstanding consultants who have made it. But this book is not for those people. It is about laying down the basics that will get newly-minted solo workers up and running, whether you are an accountant looking to change your lifestyle, a working mother who wants to work from home instead of facing the daily commute, or even an employee who has negotiated a work from home deal. All of those people YOU need a plan, a reason to get up in the morning and go to work – even if it is (temporarily) done at the kitchen table.

My whole independent career has been about having a plan and sticking to it. Getting up in the morning and knowing what I want to do that day. Yes, I am the first to admit that it doesn't always work out quite the way you planned, but if you don't have that plan you have nothing. If you are going to be a successful independent consultant you have to know where you are going and why, and be prepared to change as you have to and as conditions in the market change.

The ones that fail in this business are the ones who don't have a goal. I know – or should I say knew – too many consultants who came to consulting on the back of a big pay-out package from their former employer. What they did was 'play' at consulting. They never 'got' it. One built a horse stable in Kent and spent all their time there, occasionally calling me up to moan that there wasn't any business out there. Well, there was business, he just wasn't looking for it in any kind of planned way. And without the plan – whatever that plan is – it won't happen. If he had agreed with himself, 'Well I want to work three days a week, now what do I have to do to make that work?', he would have been organised. Galloping around a field with a mobile phone in your belt isn't prospecting for work. Neither is rubbing down a horse while making prospect calls. Amateurs are amateurs because they do it for fun, and they won't succeed.

Another had a similar experience. She was 'encouraged' to leave the cosseted confines of the corporation where she had been for 20-plus

Tip! Consulting isn't fun – it's business. Don't understand that and you don't get fed – simple.

years. She never realised how to get into the right frame of mind to be a consultant. She expected work to arrive in her lap. It doesn't: it's hard work getting work. She never found a way to translate the great talents she deployed inside a big business into those of a valued external adviser. The upshot of this was that after a miserable 24 months or so she got herself re-hired. When we meet we just don't talk about it. No plan, no enthusiasm and, sad to say, no talent for the role. Before you leap out of a cosy corporate corner, consider long and hard if it is the move for you.

Today, it doesn't matter if your plan is to work one, two, three or even seven days a week, as long as you know it and you know how to plan for it. That is what being independent is all about. As long as you know what you're doing, you've got a big chance of making it. As long as you make sure that the one day a week you've decided you want to work (lucky you!) is for that assignment, task whatever, that's fine. It's footling about, playing at being a consultant, that just doesn't work – ever.

And that, obviously, involves how much you want to earn. There is absolutely nothing wrong with saying, 'I only want to earn X', if that is what satisfies you. Independent consultants are not like those of the big firms, trying to maximise every hour. Many of us do our 'jobs' for a variety of reasons (see above), so it is not all about just making money. Most professionals I know – the ones, incidentally, who are the most successful – are doing what they do because they like it (or love it). The money is nice too, but secondary. Sure you need the basics to be in place: but most solo operators I know are doing it because they want to or because it affords them the right kind of lifestyle (which is more than monetary reward).

> *Tip! If it's only about money, think again. Successful consultants enjoy their work, profit comes second.*

Now let's look at some of the real issues that any aspiring independent consultant would do well to consider long and hard before taking the leap into what (at best) is an alternative lifestyle.

Are you an entrepreneur?

Do you think of yourself as an entrepreneur, and dream of being on the cover of *Fortune* or *Business Week*? Are you a closet Bill Gates or Richard Branson? You are? Well, too bad for you. You'll never make an independent consultant. You see, entrepreneurs want to create stuff for themselves, want to build a business and get lots and lots of other people to help them do it. Independent consultants want exactly the opposite. They want to stay small and stay – for the most part – in the background. Success for the independent consultant is a job done well (which the client usually takes the credit for!).

That's where the buzz for the solo consultant comes: telling big companies that ought to know better how to do it. Thinking around that, I imagine the world's most successful independent consultant ever was Peter Drucker, adviser to many of the most successful and powerful corporate chieftains. He always worked alone, never had an office, and if you called you usually got his wife, Doris.

Drucker didn't know it – perhaps he was too occupied with changing the corporate world – but he is the model of the successful independent consultant of the twenty-first century. Front, as in a fancy office, has been replaced today by an office in the garden or the attic; the secretary, by a bank of electronic gismos and your partner or children. It is a more relaxed – and in fact more productive – environment. One of my great friends, who was consulting from Belgium to some of the world's greatest corporations, used to scare new callers to his home when his sons conspired to put 'unusual' messages on his answerphone, usually accompanied by ghastly, ghostly music or the latest heavy metal hit. Such was his competence no one ever complained (at least not directly to him).

So successful consultants aren't entrepreneurs. Yes, they need to know how to sell, but they don't need that 'stack 'em high and sell 'em cheap' sort of mentality. Independent consultants are just that, solo operators hired for a competence that is either unique and therefore valuable, or in short supply in their client's business. (For those who need to know quickly, how to sell comes in Chapter 4.)

The multitasking megastar

Because they are not entrepreneurs, solo professionals need one big talent, which breaks into a lot of pieces. They need the ability:

- to work for and please three, four or more clients at the same time
- to be CEO, CMO, CFO, R&D director, CIO and then the rest at a moment's notice.

In my 25 years of doing this stuff, I have not met many consultants who do all these things very well. Most of us get by and then are very good at, hopefully, the key things. While there's a lot more about how to do these tasks later in the book, knowing how to 'budget' your time to get the best result takes practice. When you have client A shouting down the phone ('They wanted it in Chicago yesterday, but we only just got the data'), while you are finishing off an urgent report ('If we get this wrong we'll all get fired') for client B, all the time knowing that you haven't begun the proposal to client C and that your accountant wants your quarterly files for the VAT return (and you had promised to get that promotional e-mail out and meet with your IT expert), don't whine. Get on with it! Believe me, this scenario is better than the alternative of waiting for the phone to ring, e-mail to pop up or fax (who has one these days anyway?) to appear while rubbing down your horse in the stable.

You can look at it another way. If you are really bad at something in the long shopping list of needs to be a successful solo player, farm it out to someone who's good at it. My belief is: get the basics right, and then buy the rest at the best price you can afford. However, in start-up mode, try, try, try to do it all yourself. You don't want extraneous costs outside of good accounting and legal advice.

Ultimately, what you cannot do is get someone to replace you. In the great scheme of things, you are all you've got. If you lack motivation, find it difficult to work on your own, hate meeting people, can't communicate and can't 'ask for the order', you won't get very far. While there may be courses that can give you some help, most successful independent consultants have these skills in natural abundance, and know how to use them. If you are the kind of person who has been 'fed' work for their entire career and has never had to present or create a proposal, you may well need to think again, or put off going solo until you have gained experience (the other alternative is to work in a large consulting firm where your limitations in certain areas may never be noticed). None of us is good at everything. For example, I hate to make 'cold calls' even

if I have what I consider a good reason to do so. On the other hand, I'll go and knock on anyone's door, happy to meet face-to-face (this is probably

Tip! If you can't sell and can't ask for the order – you'll starve. Simple as that.

lucky for me as I may have ended up as a telesales consultant instead!). So each of us has hang-ups, phobias and things we are plain not good at. What we need is a score sheet that when added up gives us a more than two-thirds chance of succeeding. And a large part in achieving this – I can't stress this too much – is being able to build an effective, dynamic network that can help drive your business.

How's your network?

Chances are that if you are headed for a life in the solo lane, you've been attending a lot of networking events. Well good for you! Only one problem. In my experience, the people who attend network events are people like you, looking to cut loose and set up in business on their own. Go to most of these events and what you'll end up with is a pocket full of business cards with titles on them like managing director, managing partner and senior associate. All of them are one-, two- and three-man bands. Networking events are where people go to lie to each other about how well they are doing. If everything they tell you were true, they wouldn't be there but sunning themselves on an atoll somewhere in the Caribbean. I was once at a chamber of commerce event in a certain city (taken as a guest), and I was the only person there who wasn't a recruitment consultant!

So when I ask the question, 'How's your network?', I mean *yours*. The personal one built up and lovingly maintained like a classic car over many years. That is the network, and if you don't have one like that, you are fooling yourself (see 'Who loves ya baby?' on p. 22).

Your network is your key, your lifeline, your father confessor. If you don't have a real one then give in. It cannot be manufactured or bought. It is the result of many years of careful nurturing.

Too many would-be independent operators also make the mistake of believing that their network equals sales opportunities. Wrong. In fact, I'll add to that – VERY wrong. While your experiences might be different, while I may use my network to help me find opportunities, they rarely give me any direct business. The power of endorsement is what you need. 'You need to talk to Mike about that, he's done a lot of work in that area.' That's what networks are for. And if you have to pay a little homage in the form of a percentage, who cares?

And, as you begin to get into the idea of going it alone, realise that you have more than one network. Oh yes you have. There's a central one that possibly has fewer than a dozen close people. After that are another 20, 30 or 40 good contacts. Beyond that, there is another, comprising everyone who has ever given you a business card and whose e-mail address you therefore 'own'.

> Tip! If you are not a natural networker, admit it. Look at your contact list and ask yourself honestly: what can it do for you?

Good networks, depending on what you plan to do in this independent world, start with the basics: mum, dad, sister, brother, old school pals, Uncle Charlie. Because, whether you like it or not, they are close and they know stuff. Networks need to know stuff, that's what they are for. It is absolutely no use being able to say, 'I have this huge network of people I know', if they can't help you or don't really know who you are. If you bumped into them in the dying hours of a professional conference or at a trade show, they just don't count. Again, in the need to be honest stakes, have a real look at your 'network': just who are they and what will they ever do for you?

If you are going to succeed as an independent, you need a network that lives, breathes and can do things or get things for you. It started years ago. You are a junior solicitor, accountant, art director, or personnel executive, and when Fred and Frieda leave, you stay in touch. When Bill heads for the big break at MegaCorp, you stay in touch. When you move departments or jobs, you stay in touch. Your laptop, palmtop or Rolodex becomes your bible. In times of trouble it is a comfort to know it is there. Always up-to-date (oh yeah!) and ready to come to the rescue. Networks are dynamic, they change and evolve, but if they are to work you must devise ways to keep them current and stay in touch.

And other people's networks are your networks too. You need an introduction to company X: who can help you? If you have a real network, you can use their networks. Think of it this way: if you have just 50 people who you can call on the phone and say 'Hi', and they each have 50 people in their networks, that's a network of 2,500 people. That should keep most of us out of trouble for a while.

So a quick bit of advice here. If you are planning to go solo, sit down and list your primary and secondary networks and then throw in the rest. Then honestly ask yourself, 'What can these people do for me?' If it is nothing, be charitable and keep sending them a New Year's card (well you never know where they might end up: George Bush got made president, didn't he?). But if they look promising, call them. Yes, pick up the phone – they don't need another bloody e-mail in their lives, do they? Find reasons to talk (there's a lot more on this in Chapter 3). Keep that real network valid and up-to-date. For me, it has been a lifeline that I attend to assiduously.

Tip! Going to a network event is not networking. That's just looking at other sad souls who don't have a real network (real networkers – of course – are too busy to be there).

Well done auntie

When I wrote that line above about Uncle Charlie being part of your network, several readers of the manuscript laughed. Not funny though – serious. One of my best friends got the biggest break of his solo career from his Aunt Margaret. He told her what he was about to do and she just happened to have a regular golf partner whose husband was the chairman of a major construction company. A week later he had an assignment that took him around the world. Ten years on, he still does it.

A friend of mine tended his network garden from the comfort of a senior corporate financial position, maintaining a card file in his home study. When he took, or was 'helped' to take, early retirement, he invited all his major customers to a farewell party (the company he was 'retiring' from paid for it too!) and he picked up three assignments to act as an internal financial policeman – he's still doing it.

You don't get that sort of deal talking to like-minded people at a network club. What you want are people with completely different brains, jobs, problems and issues. Or preferably people with very few brains at all. What we all need to remember is that the independent consultant has to pray each day that organisations will continue to do what they have since the Industrial Revolution – to make big mistakes. If they really knew how to manage they wouldn't need you.

Finally, there is the other part of your network – the part you give business to. Thinking of going it alone? Well, get to know where you will find the best accountant, best IT adviser, best solicitor and so on. As you create your office (we will come to office set-ups and planning in Chapter 3) you will need these people, so get to know them before you need them. It pays off big-time. Just think, your electricity supply goes out: your IT infrastructure collapses. Do you know the electrician, the IT expert? You know, the one who will put you to the top of his call list so you can get it up and working again within an hour? If you don't, you need to. Today's world runs on technology – or it doesn't run at all.

The Old Boy's Club

The greatest networks ever are the ones that you can't buy your way into. They are comprised of the former employees of some of the world's major corporations. The concept is that employees have reunions, and as they move from country to country they join the local 'club'. Some are actually sponsored by the ex-employee's firm (who believe that it helps business). If you are into one of these, it can be a goldmine. It is an opportunity to meet a successful group of former colleagues in a relaxed atmosphere. Does business get done? Of course it does. I have a long-time headhunter pal who built his entire business on the back of belonging to three of these. Three! That's a licence to print money.

'Network, network, network' is a mantra that needs repeating. I estimate that I add a name a day, and probably remove one too. I have 548 people on my e-mail list, a good 300 of whom I can call for one thing or another. So let us use my earlier equation on that. If everyone that I feel comfortable calling (those

300) have the same number of 'live' contacts as I do, then my secondary net-work becomes 90,000. Enough said?

Well, almost. Just a final rant on this network thing. Even if you have a job in an organisation, real networking is vital. Too many people call me up and say, 'I just got fired, do you know any headhunters?' These are people who never ever call you back while they have jobs, because they are too busy. What I tell them is that the time to get to know a headhunter is when you *have* a job, not when it's too late. So even if you picked up this book at your son-in-law's office, take heed. Real networks are priceless: for everything else, there's MasterCard.

One more thing. You can, once established, consider setting up your own net-work. I did it and it is very rewarding. (For how to do it, see pp. 102–103.)

What about money?

When taking the plunge into solo swimming, the part of the plan that takes on the most crucial aspects is the financial one. While we will deal in detail with the financial implications of being a solo consultant in Chapter 6 (where my own accountant Peter Clegg takes a long hard look at what you need to consider), there are some basic points to be made here.

I don't know anyone who has succeeded in any professional activity as an independent operator who didn't have a guaranteed cash flow before they began. And the word to stare at here is 'guaranteed'. Promises are no good at all – you can't eat them.

The upside is that for most of us working as independent consultants the actual cost of getting started is relatively low. If you are doing it on the cheap, a phone line, broadband, laptop, desk and filing cabinet will get you started (there are options and scenarios in Chapter 3). But, that apart, don't try to simply wing it and hope some money comes in. Sure, spend your redundancy cash (half of it would be more sensible), but also save up, or get an iron-clad contract that delivers money into the bank on dates agreed.

My view – we are not manic, success-driven entrepreneurs remember – is that you don't need a loan, you can get going with very little to begin with if you are careful about budgeting. Having said that, it isn't really just 'to begin with': the secret of an effective and successful independent operation is to keep your expenses (your outgoings) as low as possible.

But sorting out your cash flow is vital. To use my own example: when I started I had a two-year contract with my former employer that paid monthly. What I did – I cannot believe how sensible I was! – was to live off the money from that contract and bank anything else I made. The result was that at the end of the two years I had a healthy bank balance (leased Mercedes here I come).

While start-up costs for an independent can be kept to a minimum, you have to take into account all sort of contingencies that may arise. 'Opportunity costs' – having to travel at your own expense in the hope of landing a piece of business; the possibility of having to delay delivery due to a sudden illness (even non serious illness like flu); or a client paying you later than planned. All these can hit hard at the cash flow (I, and every other solo operator, know this only too well). But if you have no cash, it is little comfort to know others have been there before you. So, money in the bank (yours, not theirs) not only brings peace of mind: it helps you operate to the maximum of your capacity.

A final tip. If cash flow is important, then more important still is invoicing. If you don't bill you don't get paid. I have known many independents in start-up mode, who get so swept up in the execution of work that they forget to send out invoices (few solo workers actually enjoy preparing fee and expense invoices), which can do more to ruin cash flow than anything else.

Home alone?

Most of us must remember the movie *Home Alone* (even if some of you were possibly the same age as the star Macaulay Culkin), which tells the story of a young boy accidentally left behind by his parents in the family home over Christmas. Well, when you throw away the security blanket of job, work colleagues and the rest, you'll know just how he felt. Hopefully, you'll also be able to take your revenge as he did, and the last scene will be a long and happy one.

But taking that big step is daunting, because for the first time you are moving out of the known world. Interestingly enough, no one seems to be able to explain why some people succeed and some people don't. Psychologists will tell you all sorts of things about people who are self-starters, brimful of self-confidence. They may be, but that isn't the secret. Others will talk of people with great technical skills that will always be in demand. But if no one knows where you are and how to contact you, that won't work either. The old adage of 'Build a better mousetrap and the world will beat a path to your door' doesn't really work unless there are a lot of signs pointing to where the door is. Of course, self-belief goes a long, long way, but without some sort of workspace it won't take you very far.

So the first thing that anyone contemplating the life of an independent consultant needs to consider is just how and where are they going to work. While we are going to address these issues in detail in Chapter 3, anyone contemplating working as an independent needs to start out with a clear idea of how he or she is going to set up the work environment.

For example, can you work from home? If you have a partner and children, that may be difficult unless you can create a 'no go' area where you can work undisturbed. I know an independent psychologist working from home who has a room that has been especially soundproofed, with a dedicated external entrance, so that she can carry out confidential discussions with her clients. No one is allowed in that room under any circumstances at any time. A freelance film director I know has his studio in his house. He has five children and none of them have ever been in his 'office', even though there are many weird and wonderful gadgets to be discovered.

Dedicated rules

It is all about setting rules for yourself and sticking to them. I work from a home office across the driveway from my house. My young son has 'visiting time' when he comes in from school, and at weekends we explore together at Daddy's desk. But when I am in full work mode on a project, he knows that it is not a place for him. When I wrote my last book, the dedication on the inside flap read, 'To my son Cameron, who resisted visits to 'Daddy's Office', except for bringing the six o'clock *verre du vin*.'

Once those rules are established it makes life a lot easier for everyone. Think about it. If you were going to work in a business, you wouldn't take the wife and kids with you, would you? It's the same here. As we will examine later, how you set yourself up in terms of physical space often depends on circumstances, location and budget (especially in the early years). But setting rules and sticking to them can make up for a lack of physical space.

Dress for success

It doesn't matter how weird or bizarre it might seem to others either, do it your way. An acquaintance of mine, who set up a thriving personal coaching business from his home, found that he actually missed going to work. What he did, much to the amusement of the neighbours, was leave home each morning, stroll down to the bus stop and back, and then begin work. For the record, he also dressed in a suit and tie everyday as it made him feel 'more businesslike'. The advice to take from this is, if it works for you, do it.

Incidentally, few people who have been on the Monday to Friday commute really have any idea what goes on at home during the so-called work hours.

To their alarm the novice home alone independent quickly discovers that distractions can come in a variety of shapes, sizes and disguises. Newly 'free' home workers report that they had no idea what went on in their neighbourhood. Mail delivery, special delivery, couriers, catalogues, passing salespeople, market researchers, gardeners and a hundred and one other sources of distraction all make a bee-line for the home worker. For others, noisy neighbours and their children are a bane to their hoped-for productivity. One of my friends reports that her neighbour still doesn't understand that she works from home, and invites her for a coffee most days to make her feel better until she gets a new job! So rules are paramount if you are to get anything done.

Then again, the opposite can apply too. There are those of us who can find working alone – especially if they have little need to travel – very limiting. No one to share your coffee break with. No one to go to lunch with. No one to share ideas with. In these cases, it is a good idea to consider some sort of office sharing arrangement. With so many people becoming independents these days, even the smallest town seems to have some dedicated office space to suit the solo operator. Often these have shared services (like photocopying, bookkeeping, and IT support) and can provide the necessary 'buzz' and collegial atmosphere that many people need from the working environment.

The perils of partnership

Of course, some people do not feel comfortable working on their own – even in a shared office arrangement – and need a work colleague with whom to share their hopes and fears, ideas and opportunities. While deciding to work with someone else – or a group of people – can seem like a great idea, be cautious before you commit too much. Time is not only a great healer but a great destroyer of relationships (especially work-related). While we examine the legal aspects of creating partnerships and companies and the like in Chapter 6, here are a few words of wisdom.

Over the years I have seen the collapse of dozens of partnerships that, on the surface at least, seem based on sound concepts. And, in most cases, it is not that familiarity breeds contempt, but that the reasons for establishing the partnership, and the personalities involved, change over time. For some obscure reason we imagine that partnerships and other legally constituted working relationships (companies, networks) continue forever without much needing to be changed. The irony is that many of us earn our living by helping companies to evolve and develop, while we ourselves just continue along with the same tired, inappropriate model. Should we be surprised then when things fall apart?

My view is that there are very few partnerships that will stand the test of time. Many are put together as an 'escape plan' from another firm, or as a way of exiting a company. Others are the result of the coming together of like-minded (at the time) people. All I would say as a piece of advice – based on long observation – is: think hard and make sure that the legal and financial processes are all in place to guard your future. The happiest independent consultants I know are those who work alone. They may have loose alliances, they may have great networks, they may have business colleagues who pass them business (and they may well give it out too), but they keep control of their own destiny. And what this does is allow YOU to make your own choices about where to take the business next.

Let me give you two examples to illustrate what I mean.

Independents are really loners

First, because there is nothing like your own experience, I have been there myself. Yes, I took on a partner. I had a business that at one time employed in one way or another upwards of 15 people. However, it was MY business: I owned it 100 per cent. At a certain point I wanted to diversify my own activities – not the least in writing books – so wanted someone to help run the operation. It seemed to me only right to give them a stake (in this case one-third) in the business. Although this person, who became the junior partner, had worked with me for some years, working as an employee is very different. Basically our ideas of the business differed: we were at different stages of our lives, and I wanted to move on to other challenges. The outcome was that we parted company. The longer term conclusion is that I would never, ever do it again. In hindsight I realised the mistake: after 15 years running my own show, I should have kept it that way. Independent consultants are just that – independent. All the good ones are autocratic and just want to get on with what they do best.

Changing people, changing times

Some years ago, I met a group of five young professionals. Enthusiastic, full of energy, of a similar age and background, they were all working for a large consulting firm. Over lunches, dinners and late night drinks they hatched *that* plan, as countless groups before and after them have done: 'Let's go and work together, let's be independent.' They did. They were a success – for about three years. Then something happened: they didn't notice, but the dynamics that had brought them together and made them succeed had slowly and subtly changed. When the five began their 'group indie' existence they were all single, practically all of one mind. Three years on one was married with children; one had been married and divorced; the third had inherited a large amount; another had married into a lot of money; and the fifth had developed a golf mania. They broke up. It was like a bright star that had shone for a while and then exploded into pieces, scattering the talent. Five years after they broke apart two of them are successful again as independent consultants. We talk about it sometimes and they realise that any partnership, whether it be with two, three, or more people, changes and will always change. Fail to move it along or accommodate the needs of all the partners and you destroy the reasons for having it in the first place.

My advice is no matter how good it looks on paper, consider long and hard if it is the right thing to do. I suggest that a full partnership at start-up is 90 per cent doomed from the outset. If you want to go that way, work as independents for a while (pool costs for office space and equipment if that makes sense), but keep your independence until you see how the relationships develop.

Bring in the professionals

Most of this chapter has been devoted to 'Should I do it? Have I the contacts, the enthusiasm, the attitude, the financial base to make it work?' Even if you think you have and your friends think it is a good idea too, my advice is that you need to make another stop before you can tick all the boxes – talk to the professionals.

You are considering becoming an independent consultant, dispensing advice and counsel for a fee. People come to you because you offer them expertise that they don't have. Well, my thought is that before you hasten out to buy that brass plaque to screw to the front door, check out your plans, ideas and attitudes with other professionals. If you can get it for free great; if not don't hesitate to pay for it. It will be worthwhile.

What you need are personal, financial and professional assessments.

First, meet with an accountant and explain your plans. Get the detail of what you want to do out into the open. What will it cost to start up (realistically)? Should you incorporate? What will it cost to run the business?

Second, talk to some people around the area you are going to work in. Do you have anything unique to offer? Is the marketplace crowded? What are the fee levels? What's the next 'big' thing?

Finally, get some sort of personality survey done. These are – I find – frighteningly accurate. If part of the survey suggests that you don't like meeting people and you are not very assertive, think it over and plan your next move.

Tip! You are planning to be a professional. So be professional and take the advice of those who know. It is invaluable. And another thing, get into the habit of doing this as you progress in your career. Check out your plans, re-assess yourself, make your accountant (even your bank manager!) your friend and confidante.

This is really important, because the other thing you need before you can get going is someone (preferably a few people) you can turn to when the going gets tough.

Shoulders to cry on

There is a song called 'When the going gets tough, the tough get going'.[3] Sounds good with a guitar background. Unfortunately it's just another myth. In the real world, when the going gets tough, we look for a shoulder to cry on – or its equivalent. What everyone – and I do mean everyone – needs are easy-to-reach sources of sympathy. We all make mistakes and unforced errors, and are victims of other people's screw-ups too. It is at these times that we need to be able to turn to people who can help out. These are the Samaritans of the solo worker. And I do think you need more than one.

Why? Well, sometimes you just need sympathy. Someone who cares about you unconditionally. It could be your old school friend, college chum, drinking buddy, brother, sister or even your mother or father. A person who won't point the finger at you, who won't stir up those 'It was all my fault!' fears. Every independent should have these people, who have to be on hand and easy to reach when you need them (hopefully not often!). Sympathy through text messages doesn't really cut it.

But you also need someone who's been there before you, and knows the professional issues as well. Who is able to offer sound advice and counsel, and has possibly faced the same problems. Maybe he or she knows from bitter experience how things should have been done differently. Now you can learn from that.

When we work for big business, we have work colleagues we can talk to, possibly even sympathetic bosses or supervisors. On your own, you need a replacement set of those work colleagues. The trick to being alone is never really to be alone. Help and succour are just a phone call away.

Ideally your professional 'shoulder' will really understand your dilemmas, because they have worked in similar environments as you – probably not doing the same sort of work, but with the same profile of clients. This makes them an ideal sounding board.

I have a great friend of mine who has always been my shoulder to cry on. He always seems to have the right answer, usually because he has experienced the same thing and knows exactly what to say. This relationship is basically

[3] 'When the going gets tough, the tough get going.' Billy Ocean, 1986.

one way, as he never seems to ask my advice (probably because I have brought him too many problems over the years): but there are others that are very much two-way. Not only do these people make a very useful cushion for your fears, but they are also the pressure valve that can relieve tension when you finally resolve the situation and add it to your library of 'war stories'.

Of course, there is another thing that you need to possess in order to survive as an independent: a nose for trouble.

Can you smell trouble?

I've been pretty lucky in my working life. Most of the clients I have worked for have been major corporations, consulting firms and institutions. Obviously, not all independent consultants are going to have a portfolio of clients like that. If you are working nationally, or within a region of a country, chances are that your business will be based around the local private and public sector. However, whether you are working for a Fortune 500 firm or the local town council, knowing that you are going to get paid is critical. Later (in Chapter 7) we'll look at the politics of payment, but for now, suffice to say: rely on your nose to smell out trouble.

Usually turning it down – before it turns you over – is just a matter of how you feel about the project and how the coffers are looking. But, every time I smelled trouble it was there. I knew an old advertising professional who used to say, 'You step on a dog turd and you maybe can't see it right away, but it doesn't take long before it starts to smell.' That is sound advice. People who ask for more than they need; people who change the brief; people who are late with the first payment having said that 'money is not the issue here'. All of them are suspect right away. And the one that is the dead give-away is the potential client who says, 'You know, our product is so good that we want to give you a part of the profits. If you work for us, we'll give you a percentage of everything we sell: of course we won't pay you anything until we sell something.' That is how to get poor fast. Also watch out for those who come back to you and try and cut your budget halfway through when you are already committed. Get out FAST. Things will only get worse.

There is an old saying, 'If it looks too good to be true it probably is.' Hang it over your desk, tattoo it on your arm or whatever. Just don't forget it.

Who loves ya baby?

I thought that to end this chapter it would be good to list some of the myths of our solitary profession. Many of these are based on my own experiences, others have been provided by friends and work colleagues. The reason for doing it here is to act as a warning. Rather like cigarette packets, independent consulting should come with a warning notice. It may not kill you, but it can leave you severely bruised, depending on how often you fall down! If you are still determined to make it on your own, read on, we are only just getting started.

What they don't tell you at any business school on the planet earth about independent consulting – and why would they?

- All the people (yes, *all*) the people who ever said, 'When you go independent we'll give you work' never, ever do.
- All your 'friends' who you gave work to when you had a 'real' job never answer your calls, e-mails or texts.
- You have *one* chance to set your fees: never lower them, you'll never get them back up again – ever.
- Anyone who asks you to speak for free as it is a 'great network opportunity' is lying. Why would you want to speak to a group of people who are all sitting in front of you earning their salary for being there?
- People do not always tell you they have decided to cancel your meeting. Always, always confirm before you go and remember you are at the very bottom of the food chain.
- The 'buzz' of feeling wanted is a curse you need to get over. Learn to turn work down.
- Guard your intellectual property with your life! Don't give it to clients. Give them ideas, not the whole encyclopaedia.
- Potential clients can and do steal. Never write a proposal so detailed that they don't need you to implement it.

Checklist 1: The go-it-alone checklist

My advice is work your way through this and to be very, very honest with yourself (if you get to this point it is getting serious). Also, get two or three of your friends either to complete it, assessing how effective you think you would be as an independent operator, or at least to discuss it with you before you go any further.

Do you think of yourself as a work-alone self-starter, and do have you any proof that you are?

yes					no
5	4	3	2	1	0

Do you have any business that you can pick up (guaranteed) immediately?

yes					no
5	4	3	2	1	0

Will you have to borrow money from a bank, or friends and relatives?

yes					no
5	4	3	2	1	0

Do you really, genuinely, enjoy your chosen profession?

yes					no
5	4	3	2	1	0

Do you like to play golf, go fishing, go drinking Saturdays and Sundays, and will you miss it if you can't do it?

yes					no
5	4	3	2	1	0

Are you ready to invest in technology to help you, do you know enough about the available hardware and software and do you have a good supplier/maintenance firm?

yes					no
5	4	3	2	1	0

Can you be a 'Jack of all trades' and do things you would not have done as an 'executive' or employed professional and that might seem below your previous status?

yes					no
5	4	3	2	1	0

Can you work long hours without immediate payback?

yes					no
5	4	3	2	1	0

Can you juggle work so that all your clients get the full attention they think they deserve?

yes					no
5	4	3	2	1	0

Are you able to keep a focus on what you do best and not be distracted from your main goal?

yes					no
5	4	3	2	1	0

Are you able to be a CEO, strategist, marketer, HR manager, financial director, receptionist and your own PA all rolled into one, every day, 365 days a year?

yes					no
5	4	3	2	1	0

Can you honestly sell yourself and your services, not once but every day, and enjoy doing it?

yes					no
5	4	3	2	1	0

Can you maximise and extend your network every day, and sell every day while you are working on client business (in other words can you multitask three, four, five things at once)?

yes					no
5	4	3	2	1	0

Can you ignore the wrong sort of criticism, and still believe that you are the best?

yes					no
5	4	3	2	1	0

Can you lose clients, pick yourself up and go and find some more, and keep doing it?

yes					no
5	4	3	2	1	0

Are you capable of continually evaluating your business and doing what's right for the future, seeing and building on new opportunities?

yes					no
5	4	3	2	1	0

Do you have good, trustworthy suppliers (lawyers, accountants, IT specialists etc.) who will go the extra mile for you?

yes					no
5	4	3	2	1	0

Can you smell trouble and do you have an instinct for bad business deals?

yes					no
5	4	3	2	1	0

Now, on the basis of your responses, do you really think you should take this idea further?

If the answer is 'yes' then you need to assess your personal circumstances.

Checklist 2: Check out yourself

Just how flexible are you? More to the point perhaps, how difficult would it be to make a major change to your lifestyle/workstyle? Without understanding that, it really is impossible to think about starting life as an independent consultant with any hope of lasting success.

1 Your current status

- Are you financially secure enough to launch a career as an independent consultant? _____

- How much of a financial cushion do you have? _____

- Do you have a pension and can you still pay into it? _____

- Do you have a partner with a job? Is it a secure job? _____

- Would your partner help you out with tasks associated with your new work (administration, answering phones etc.)? _____

- Are you and your partner compatible to do this in a work environment? _____

- Do you have children? Are they still living with you? _____

- Do you have elderly dependents to consider now/ in the near future? _____

- How important is the community you live in to you (family, friends, local associations etc.)? _____

Based on your responses, write down your present status:

_____

_____

_____

_____

_____

_____

_____

2 Your financial situation

- Do you own your house? _____

- What level of income do you need to maintain your basic lifestyle?_____

- Could you make do with less money?_____

- Can your partner's income provide for basic needs until you get fully established? _____

- Are your children (if any) still at school (do you pay school fees) or going through college/university? _____

- Do you have elderly dependents and their attendant costs to consider now/in the near future? _____

- What assets do you have (pensions, stocks, other savings and holdings)? _____

- What assets would you be prepared to sacrifice, put at risk to get the business operational? _____

- What liabilities do you have?_____

- Have you discussed your financial situation with a professional financial adviser? _____

Based on your responses, write down your current and likely future financial status:

_____

_____

_____

_____

_____

_____

_____

_____

_____

_____

_____

_____

_____

3 Your health

- Have you had a medical check-up in the last 12 months? _____
- Has your partner had a medical check-up in the last 12 months? _____
- Are you capable of a high (mental) stress job? _____
- Could you put up with a heavy workload, early mornings and late nights?_____
- Could you put up with uncertainty about your future success and income? _____
- How would your partner/children feel about this? _____

Based on your responses, write down your current health status and how it affects your future plans:

_____

_____

_____

_____

_____

_____

_____

_____

_____

_____

_____

_____

_____

4 Things you really like to do

What are your favourite parts of your work/professional life?

_____

_____

_____

_____

_____

_____

What are your favourite parts of your personal life?

_____

_____

_____

_____

_____

_____

Which of these favourite parts would you be prepared to give up if you had to?

_____

_____

_____

_____

_____

_____

_____

Which of these favourite parts would you not be prepared to give up, under any circumstances?

_____

_____

_____

_____

_____

_____

_____

Based on all your answers, write down a frank, honest assessment of where you, your partner and your family stand today, and what you would and would not do to get into an independent work-style.

Example One: 'I am a totally free agent, exceptionally healthy with no close commitments. I would enjoy the challenges of being an independent consultant. I don't mind late nights and unsociable hours of work or considerable travel. Additionally, I have a financial cushion (or a signed contract for guaranteed work) that will cover my outgoing for at least six to 12 months.

My pastimes are those that allow me the maximum amount of flexibility, and I can give or put aside nearly all of them if I need to.'

Example Two: 'Being honest, my sense of home and family – as well as the local community – are the most important things to me. I have a partner with a secure, but low-paying job, which she enjoys, my children are practically through college and I really don't want to go into the stress of trying to survive as an independent at this time.'

_____

_____

_____

_____

_____

_____

_____

_____

_____

_____

_____

_____

_____

_____

_____

Chapter 2

How to get started

Don't compromise yourself. You're all you've got.

Janis Joplin

You've got to take the bitter with the sour.

Sam Goldwyn

Well congratulations! You have decided, even after all the discouragement of Chapter 1, to go out and do it. Your days as an employee or a student are numbered. You've checked out all the angles, know who you are, what you want to do and how to get yourself there. But remember one big thing before we begin. Now you are committed the thing you need most of all to get you on your way and sustain you is enthusiasm and self belief. You have to leave all those nagging little doubts behind and get on with the show.

While there is no one I have ever met who made the transition to a solo career without some trepidation, they have all had a strong motivation to succeed. But again, it has been the planning of the process that has had the biggest impact on their future success. In Chapter 1 we touched on what assets you need – both physical and mental – to begin the great adventure. Now we are going to look at the transitional process itself. What's the best way to begin?

To start off with, I offer some examples of different types of people, all aiming to make an independent career, and take you through the first steps of the transition process. From there, we get into more of the detail of the daily process and what needs to be in place to make it work. The reason for doing it this way is simple: today, there are so many options and choices that the term 'independent consultant' covers an ever-broadening range of people and professional activity.

The escaping executive

What executive of any seniority sitting in that traffic jam or crushed in a crowded, standing room only train compartment hasn't dreamed of working for themselves at one time or another? After all, they are talented, organised, plugged into their profession. Surely, they think, there must be a better way to make a living than spending almost a day a week stuck in traffic. Well, there is. The only thing you have to consider is: what's the best way to get out?

Many companies today are beginning – albeit slowly – to realise that if they don't make it easier for their talented employees to work in other ways, they will ultimately lose them. So offering long-term contracts, part-time work opportunities and other incentives are increasing in popularity. How many options are offered depends on the age, seniority and expertise of the person about to make that choice to quit.

But there is one overriding common denominator. Assuming you are not in the firing line, you have value. Whether directly or indirectly employed, you can make a contribution. Indeed, many firms faced with hiring freezes and departmental reorganisations welcome the idea of reducing headcount while keeping the talent close through a contract to work for a certain number of days each week, month or year. Even the legendary Jack Welsh of GE cut a deal as an independent consultant, although he probably did rather better than most of us in terms of ongoing compensation!

And that is the term that you most need to concentrate on: the 'deal.' If you can get your firm to agree to fund your departure through a contract (even if it is only based on the redundancy compensation you may have got if they had ever chosen to terminate you), you are really ahead. They are funding your start-up operation.

There are some basic rules to follow to make this happen effectively and professionally.

First, carefully sound out the firm and get a feel of what their appetite is likely to be for this sort of initiative. Do they have any formal programme for this? Has anyone else ever tried it and what was the outcome?

Second, know exactly what you want in terms and conditions. There is no point in negotiating without being very clear what you will settle for (always ask for more than you really hope to get).

Third, try and make sure you have a way back if negotiations fail. It is no good cutting yourself off. Anyway, if you are going to work externally for the firm, you need to maintain their trust and their commitment to you.

Fourth, get an employment lawyer to go over the terms and conditions and conduct the final negotiations or exchange of contracts with the firm.

Not only is this more professional, but it takes the personalities out of the deal. One thing: get a contract with a renewable clause in there for six months before the first term ends. That way if they want to terminate, you'll have six months to do something about it.

Finally, exceptional circumstances apart, try and limit the amount of time you're committing. If you want to develop a business as an independent consultant, you need to have elbow room to do it.

Of course, if you can't get your firm to fund your venture, the next best thing is to get ad hoc work from them. Again, keep it professional and try and tie down some type of long-term commitment, even if it is just for a few days a month (they usually creep up). Remember, you know their business, and once on the outside you can show them what a valued asset you can be. Obviously, some executives and specialists can make easier transitions than others. Marketers, communications people, human resource specialists and IT experts often find it easier to set up on their own than financial, sales and production personnel. But there is no real barrier as long as you have a clear plan of what you want to achieve. I know a production engineer who is still working from time to time for his old company, 20 years after leaving them (he works for their competition too). Similarly, one of the best salesmen I ever met quit his job (and his excellent annual bonus) and became a freelance consultant. He didn't make as much money, but his lifestyle improved enormously.

This – of course – is what many of today's wannabe independents are looking for: a different way of life and the chance to earn a living as well. Getting out of that daily commute can increase productivity immensely.

> ### Turning a daily commute into profit
>
> For the last 20 years I have always worked close to home: first in a second apartment in the same building, then living 'above the business' in a townhouse, and latterly in a specially built office across my garden. In every case I was able to put in two hours – at least – every day by not having to commute anywhere. Certainly you go and see people, but when you go back to the office to get things done you are already home. That makes the home working independent very, very efficient. This is something that the average employee (and employer for that matter) rarely appreciates – until they try it themselves!

This need to change careers seems to be happening more frequently. And it seems to strike young and old, junior, middle and senior management. With companies again concerned about the shortage of talent to fund their own ambitions, this should be a good time for those bent on an independent career to score. Companies need experience, and the independent provides that.

Many who have made the transition from employee to solo worker say that they relish the variety of the work. And the thing they all say they miss least? Office politics!

Can anyone do it? Can anyone make the transition from salaried employee to fee-charging independent? Here are some examples to consider.

- A 30-something corporate lawyer bailed out of her high-paid job to set up a one-woman law firm, specialising in employment law and cross-border hiring.
- A marketing director successfully transferred from working for his multi-national employer to being a one-man corporate social responsibility consultant.
- A management development executive in a major retailer became a trainer, coach and mentor to a group of small firms in a rural location, a role that gives him growing opportunities to do hands-on work.

Then again, others not only switch from employee to independent, they change their career too. Increasingly, in a world full of more and more choice in what we do, people are deciding to turn an interest, hobby or passion into an opportunity to make a living. In some locations, younger people are doing this because they feel disenchanted with the kind of life that is imposed on them by the nine-to-five grind. Recent studies show that up to 90 per cent of 30-somethings feel 'stifled by the rigours and conventions of corporate life'. Worse still for the employers facing talent famines, reports say that, 'unlike many of their predecessors, these people have the means, the mind-set and the technological savvy to do something about it.' Yes, bailing out of the corporate rat-race is becoming all too common, and it is going to increase year on year. But it isn't just the employees of big business who are choosing other options.

Consultants bail out too

Working life in a big consulting firm – or even a mid-sized one – isn't any better than that in any industrial or service business. In fact, these past years it has been a lot more precarious. Bonuses may be good in the bumper years, but there haven't been too many of them of late. To be honest, most consulting firms – whatever their business – have had serious downsizing programmes going on. The knock-on effect has been a glut of refugees from the big firms either choosing or being forced by circumstance to go it alone. And these are not the ones who failed after the first 24 months either, these are people who are well trained, well qualified and who know how to deal with clients. They are – possibly – the best equipped group to go it alone and succeed.

And I am not talking just about management consultants: far from it. They could be accountants, architects, trainers, organisational development experts, consulting engineers, coaches, IT experts ... the list is endless.

Digging for victory

I met a 30-year-old made redundant from his job in a leading architectural firm, where he had specialised in landscape design. Using his training, he moved to the country with his partner and began a one-on-one design service aimed at assisting private clients to revitalise their gardens. He has made a particular success of offering advice to nouveau riche landowners eager to spend their annual bonuses. But he has been careful to retain his consulting status, employing local builders, fencers, gardeners and tree surgeons where necessary.

And as with employees from companies, consultants can often soften the blow of their departure by getting ad hoc work from their former employer. Better still, the really smart ones seem more than able to take business with them!

Consultants from large and medium-sized firms who find themselves starting a business offer great services – their training has usually been excellent and they are very up-to-date with both techniques and technology. So buyers can pick up a highly effective, former big-time business consultant at a relatively bargain price. Therefore, if you find yourself in this position and having to sell your services, don't be shy about mentioning where you used to work: it can be a huge asset in getting your new one-person business off the ground. Indeed, if all the consultants who claim to have worked for that doyen of the consulting profession McKinsey & Co were placed end to end, I have little doubt they would reach to the moon and back!

Back-to-work spouse meets downshifter

A few years ago we probably wouldn't have needed to be quite so politically correct, but today there are quite a lot of so-called 'househusbands' who pursue not only a life of childcare and housework, but a career as well. While it used to be naturally assumed that the husband would be the focaccia-winner, today's climate is different. Technology coupled with the increasingly flexible working options that employers are offering mean that it is easier than ever for both parents to assume some of the pleasure/burden of childcare. A woman can return to full-time employment and easily get one, two or three days a week to work at home. This allows a husband to set up a solo consulting firm and still be able to get out and visit clients and prospects. As I said in Chapter 1, all it takes is a plan.

This kind of approach works excellently for any partnership because it allows one person to work full-time, while the other takes the 'risk' of going it alone. Sensible couples I know work on the basis of living on the guaranteed monthly income and saving the consulting fees to build the business in the future. For many, this type of arrangement can have several stages.

- Stage one: Partner A quits a full-time job, and living on the income of Partner B begins to establish himself/herself as a sole trader.
- Stage two: Once partner A has established a relatively steady business model, Partner B then quits, and using the income from Partner A's consulting activity begins life as an independent as well.
- Stage three: Both reasonably established, Partners A and B then combine their talents to create a more dynamic business operation.

Having said that – and as a father of a young child and therefore a 'fan' of very early morning TV – I have noticed that in many of those so-called 'escape' programmes, there seems to be a growing tendency for a slightly different version. Please ignore my cynicism.

- Stage one: Partner A quits full-time job and moves to a rural/semi-rural location (insert country here ....) to start a (insert rural or hospitality-type occupation here ....), while Partner B keeps his or her job, lives in tiny apartment and commutes at weekends.
- Stage two: Partner A establishes business and is joined by Partner B.
- Stage three: Partners A and B sell business/land/chateau to Megacorp Inc and move back to bright lights and big city!

Well, something along those lines anyway. The point is that it is *your* choice what you want to do with your life, and people are increasingly plumping for lifestyle first and workstyle second.

As I emphasised in my recent book *The New Rules of Engagement*,[4] work–life balance is wrong: it is life–work balance that people ascribe to. Everyone has a dream of being in control, and the rules and regulations of the modern-day corporation – as I described above – don't suit today's freewheeling society.

---

[4] Johnson, M. (2004) *The New Rules of Engagement: Life-work balance and employee commitment.* London: CIPD.

Then again, you don't have to be in a partnership to take the leap into the unknown. Singletons do it too, as do single parents and those high flyers who just want to spend more time with their children or develop other interests before it is too late. In a society that celebrates –-even venerates – choice, we have become a multi-choice world. It is not surprising that an increasing number of people see being an independent as the way to 'have it all'.

That includes the downshifter. There are a thousand and one reasons people downshift. Wanting to escape the city, the arrival of children, a health scare, a death in the family, being made redundant, a sudden inheritance, getting married – the list goes on and on. Again, it is all about having a plan and sticking to it. Determined downshifters are certainly a growing force to be reckoned with. One of my favourites is the jaded management consultant who just can't take the commute and the city life anymore. He and his wife (the children had already gone their own ways) moved to a hill village in rural Spain. Three years later, he was the business consultant to the local farmer's co-operative, masterminding the branding of their excellent produce all over the world. This is the type of person who if parachuted into the middle of the Sahara would find a way to do business (camel psychology?).

The graduate

Remember the movie *The Graduate*? The famous line from the publicity posters and the book cover was: 'This is Benjamin. He's a little worried about his future.'[5] And what does he say to his dad? 'For twenty-one years I have been shuffling back and forth between classrooms and libraries. Now you tell me what the hell it's got me.'

Well Benjamin, you may be the most famous graduate of all time, but you'll be pleased to know he is not alone in feeling like that. Every year more and more graduates shun big business and the rest of the services that support it. Every year an increasing number of graduates take that gap year and never come back. Every year a growing number start their own businesses. They may not think they are 'consultants' in the true sense of the definition, but actually they are.[6] And what they 'consult' in reflects our twenty-first century habits. Like my friend the landscaper (see p. 35), I know of young, just graduated consultants in fields as varied as yacht design, sports medicine, event organisation and historic building conservation. They say that it was their inability to

[5] Webb, C. (1963) *The Graduate*. Harmondsworth: Penguin; film by United Artists, director Mike Nichols.

[6] The *Collins Concise Dictionary* defines consultant as 'a specialist who gives expert advice or information'.

get enthused by the 'adult', grey, organised world that settled their future direction.

For anyone reading this who thinks consultants wear suits and ties and have to have a degree in law or accountancy, forget it. If you've got a great idea you can do it too. You will have to work at it, but you'll have a lot of fun as well.

Most interesting is that it is often the best and the brightest that are taking this route of school, university, solo employment: fitting into, or simply creating, new independent consulting opportunities.

The early retiree

I suppose you could lump this category in with the escaping executives, but in most cases I have come across, the motivations to set up as a sole trader are different. Most have some kind of income stream (pension, investments and so on), so they are not dependent on making a lot of money. Basically, many of them do it because it keeps them occupied and gives them a goal in life. Fifty years ago, their fathers had the garden shed to potter about in; their mothers had the sewing room. Today they are offering their expertise (about their former job or their acquired pastime) for a fee. Sometimes they do it for no fee, because they like it! I know retirees who – after a long and distinguished career in business or public service – have become some of the very best specialised consultants.

- The managing director of a commercial art studio, whose pastime was Old Masters, is now one of the world's most sought after fine-art consultants.
- An IT manager, whose hobby was gothic architecture, is now a consultant to one of Spain's most historic cities.
- The head of human resources of one of Europe's leading corporations now acts as a consultant in acquiring horses for an Arab prince's stud.
- A former schoolteacher now, at the age of 65, teaches conflict negotiation to managers.
- A retired jumbo-jet captain is now the navigational consultant to one of the world's leading manufacturers of sailing craft.

All these people have taken something that was their passion – their 'escape' from the reality of earning a living – and turned it into a job that they enjoy. All of them have told me that if they had known what was going to happen they would have done it earlier. I tell them that if they had tried, they would probably have failed. They are valuable now because for years they have been acquiring the knowledge that people are willing to pay for.

But it goes to prove that you can be anything you want to be at any age. It also shows that almost anyone can be an independent consultant if that's what they have really set their minds on being. Now what we need to discuss is some of the things you need to do – and some of the things you don't need to do – as you begin to get into start-up mode.

Planning the successful start-up

What not to waste time over

If you ignore the rest of the advice in this book, or you're just in too much of a hurry to start to get through it all – READ THIS section NOW! Reason is, what follows is based on the long and sometimes bitter experiences of me and others like me. We started with enthusiasm, a little common sense (which, like a little knowledge, can be a dangerous thing in the wrong hands), some capital and not much else. We survived (well, not most of us actually), and we learned as we went along. Now it is my great pleasure to pass what we learned on to you.

The first thing to realise is that it doesn't matter who you are, what you're planning to do or which country you are living in. Special local business practices and taxes apart, what follows here and in Chapter 6 is universal in its application to the independent consultant's operational start-up and ongoing work. The areas are covered in no order of importance.

Adminfrustration

This is a word you'll adopt gladly. Unless you are a complete nerd, administration is a pain that occurs somewhere in the nether regions. So you need to find ways to deal with it in a quick, painless fashion. First piece of advice is – if at all possible – do administrative work once a week. I know lots of sole traders who do it either very early in the morning or Sunday evenings. Then you think that it is not impinging on your workday. Every business has to deal with administration of one sort or another: there is no way around it.

If you get very busy, or you travel a lot, I would recommend either having a 'helper' who comes in once a week and sorts it all out for you, or using an office services firm. Both are good ways to get your administration done without costing a lot of money. Most charge by the hour, which means that if they are not doing anything they don't cost you.

Years ago even the smallest operator seemed to have a secretary of one sort or another, who answered phones, wrote letters (this was before the PC changed all our lives), booked travel and filed everything (see below). Today, technology has made most of this largely irrelevant. You can do it all for yourself in a fraction of the time it used to take. But the administration just won't go away.

When I started a few years ago to work solo again, my accountant, Peter Clegg (whom you'll meet up with in Chapter 6), was honest enough to explain that it was useless having him or one of his highly qualified people do all my administration. He found me a bookkeeper, who came in and did basic tax returns and kept all the paper together (sorting credit card receipts was the bane of my life!). All I do is keep bank statements, travel receipts and so forth in files, and the bookkeeper comes in (usually once a month, but it can be just once a quarter) and makes sense of it all.

Others use their spouse for this task. This – assuming they don't mind it and you don't care if they get to see that you spent €300 on a dinner in Rome – can be an additional way of saving money. Another reason for engaging your spouse in tasks like this is that you can (dependent on national tax laws) pay them to do it, or have them on the board of directors. My company is incorporated in the UK, and my wife acts as the company secretary. This allows her to draw a salary and take dividends. However, it is important to know what the prevailing tax implications are about such cosy, keep-it-in-the-family arrangements. Currently in the UK, the taxman has a less than congenial view of this type of set-up.

The other thing that may well help you is to get any of your regular payments on some sort of direct debit system, so you don't spend time writing out cheques or making payments on-line. Critical items like telephone and broadband invoices need to be paid on time, and if you are out of the office for extended periods you have to make sure that all this is operational.

Another tip is to pile up all your payments and do them in one go once a month. That may sound like a very obvious thing to do, but again it takes discipline. I put a date in my diary and make sure that I take that hour to make payments.

Invoicing

It is the same with invoicing. Despite the fact that it is nice to get paid for one's labours, I have never met anyone who enjoys the drudgery of raising fee and expense invoices. But if you want to get paid on time, you have to make the time to get it done. Again, have a regular date for that. Or – if you want to avoid those tardy payers – invoice automatically as soon as you can.

Many independent consultants work on a project basis. When I work that way, I usually charge one-third up front as the project kicks-off; one-third when (say) the research process is complete; and the final third, plus an accounting of final expenses, at the end of the project. To make sure you don't end up badly out of pocket (and to keep that ever critical cash flow available), I also invoice an up-front expense fee. This is particularly important where a project involves either travel, hotels and other subsistence costs, or paying the suppliers who are supporting you.

> Tip! There was a marketing consultant who got so arrogant that he actually charged to his clients the time it took him to prepare the invoices he was sending them. This is not a good idea: especially when the client finds out. As they say, 'Don't try this at home!'

The trick in all this is very straightforward. You are NOT a bank. If you don't invoice up front the client is using your money. When you consider how long it can take to get paid these days (see Chapter 7 for more on this), it becomes a clear case of the sooner you get money in, the better.

... and the X-Files

The other part of Adminfrustration that all sane people hate is filing stuff. But once more, it is a necessary evil. Again, the best thing to do is have a tray, box, drawer or whatever and pile it up and do it all at one time. Either put a date in the diary (as above), or save it for a wet day or when a client or prospect cancels a meeting. Personally, I don't recommend getting help to do this. If you are a true independent you need to know where the material is filed and to create a system that works for you.

> ### Ooh-la-la!
>
> During my work life in Brussels I had a French-speaking secretary, who joined full of enthusiasm and fresh from secretarial college. I left on a two-week assignment and she decided that in order to learn the business, she would take my rather sad filing system and completely re-do it. 'Great', I thought, 'what an excellent idea.' On my return, I went into the office on a Saturday morning, when no one else was there, because I needed to consult some files. I couldn't find them anywhere and eventually gave up. When my new secretary appeared for work on the Monday morning I asked where was the file on printers, and the one on general suppliers. 'Under 'I' for Imprimeries and 'F' for Fournisseurs', she explained. Upside was that it helped a lot of our non-French speaking staff learn a lot of new vocabulary!

Of course, files are really there to decorate your office walls! Their principle function is to gather dust. So the other thing to do is clean them out every so often. I took this to extremes last year and hired a builder's skip. I filled it in half a day with old management books, research papers and the like.

Hoarding is OK as long as it is useful – I have materials from two decades ago that I quite often find useful. As an example, recently I was involved in a study of the key concerns of CEOs in Europe. I was able to go back to a study I had carried out in 1985 (20 years earlier) that produced some remarkable comparative data that really enhanced the new material. So when you have that office clean-out think carefully about what goes and what stays.

I tend to file by project. The best way I know to operate is to give every project you get involved with a number and create a file for that. These act as current project files (I use simple clear plastic folders), and then are just filed away when the project is complete. Ongoing projects (for example, I research and write monthly and quarterly newsletters for clients) usually have a master file that contains basic agreements, meeting discussions and ideas as well as a file for each edition of the newsletter (containing research notes and draft and final copies).

Tip! I'm old-fashioned in some things. So while I appreciate the freedom that technology has given me, I still like a piece of paper. If, like me, you tend to forget to back up your computer every Friday before you pack it in for the weekend, make sure that all those proposals and contracts and confidentiality agreements are in hard copy and filed away (preferably in a safe).

In addition, I keep client contracts, proposals and customer contracts in the client's file and in a master file as well. That way you can usually lay your hands on a copy.

Planning, pacing and patterns

The production plan

Since the first day I started working as an independent consultant (25 September 1982 to be exact), I have always run my business from a production plan. The reason for this is probably that in my employed career, most of the firms I worked for operated in that way. While in a firm a production plan helps everyone keep track of who is doing what and of meeting deadlines, it is also an invaluable aid for the solo worker. Although the idea of having a planning meeting with yourself may sound a little bizarre, it does pay off.

What I have done is to stuck rigorously to two rules:

- It *must* be updated each week (no matter where I am)
- It has to be on a single page only (which is why mine is currently in 8pt type!)

I have an electronic copy with me wherever I go, but a hard copy sits on one of the plastic document holders next to my big flat screen.

Every Monday morning (just as I did with my team for many years), I make a pot of green Japanese tea and have a planning session with myself. I find if I don't do this there are certain things I just never, ever follow up on.

Now, I call mine a production plan, and indeed it does examine the things in progress. But it is also my key aide-mémoire for the things I need to keep an eye on. From this production plan meeting with myself, I develop a to do list for that day and the week to come.

So what can you find on Mike Johnson's one-page production plan?

- **Current booked business**. These are projects that have been agreed (and given a project number, as explained earlier: see pp. 42). I add certain basic details: state of project (including those that have been completed and billed, but not yet paid: they only come off when they are paid in full!), subject for a newsletter, next client meet, deadline date, etc.
- **Business development: the critical list.**These are the projects I am currently bidding for (usually that means a proposal is under consideration), and I include information on what the project is and its current status.
- **Business development: follow-ups.** These comprise hot and not-so-hot contacts that you really need (both as possible business opportunities and also for research and network opportunities).
- **Meeting/conference commitments.** Where I am supposed to be, what I am speaking on and related issues.
- **The Futurework Forum.** Events and issues related to the network I created.
- **The percentage club.** Details of the co-workers I have business development/referral agreements with, and their current status.
- **Personal writing.** Current Mike-Johnson-only projects (like this book!).
- **Upcoming visits.** Details of people I need to contact when I travel to different cities.

Without my production plan I would be lost. Personally, I have never found another way to keep all of my activities in one place (on one page!) that is so effective. This is not a to do list, it is an easy to update summary of my professional life. Incidentally, if you keep hard or electronic copies for a period of years it is a great way to look at how your business developed and evolved, and how clients waxed and waned. A potted corporate history of your business – one page at a time.

Pacing your day

I have referred a lot already to having a plan. This equally applies to how you are going to work. One of the big dangers of going to work for yourself is that the lines between on time and off time begin to blur. If you are working from home it is all to easy to wander into your 'office' in your bathrobe at 5am because you can't sleep, do a few things at the weekend and 'just check for that e-mail' at 10pm before you turn in for the night. For some of us it doesn't matter. For others, it really is necessary to create a routine.

Swinging through the seasons

It really doesn't matter what your routine is, or if you change it. I have a golfing pal of mine who has two routines: summer and winter. In winter, he gets into the 'office' around 8am and works happily until around 12, when he stops and walks the dog. He then resumes around 1pm and works through until 5 or 6pm (later if needs be). In summer, he is in his office by 6am and stops at 1pm, when he has a light lunch and plays golf or goes sailing. Around 7pm he gets back and catches up on anything that's needed. His seasonal switch usually takes place around the time the clocks move forward or back. He's tried it the other way around in the summer, and worked in the afternoons, but has come to the conclusion that 'the action' takes place in the morning, and he can always play catch-up in the evening with anything urgent. He also spends a lot of time talking to the USA, and at 7pm UK or European time they are still very much in their working day. Advice to take: have a routine based on your business needs, not what anyone else thinks.

Although creating the basic routine is important, the pace you set is vital too. If things are quiet you can do one of two things: (1) get worried and go searching desperately for new business; (2) go and have a good lunch. I am not joking. I like what I call 'down-days', when you know that however hard you try the people you call won't be there (of course they are employees, so they are 'in a meeting'), promised material doesn't arrive, and plans take a last-minute dive into the abyss. At this point you may as well store up your energies and creative juices and head for the nearest hostelry. Strange thing is that every time I do that I take my big pad of (always yellow) legal pads and I *always* get at least one good idea. Don't sit alone and mope about, get out and see the world – it really makes a difference.

Then there is the other side of the independent consultant's coin – the day all hell breaks loose, the heavens fall in and there's a five-alarm fire burning on your desk. And this cataclysmic event always takes place the day before you go on holiday, your partner's birthday or your daughter's wedding/first school play/graduation (please choose one). My view on this is that there is always tomorrow. Go and do what you need to do (the family obligation) and then clear up the mess. You may spend the day traumatised about how you are going to pay for your daughter's wedding when you think you may have just blown the Acme Engineering account, but it seldom comes to that (honest!).

As for those days when the alarm bell rings as you are preparing to switch off the lights – well, that's show business. That's what you signed up for. At times like this it is useful to remind yourself (and your nearest and dearest too) that if you were still an employee, you wouldn't just be down the hallway or across the garden. You would still be at work. Still having to switch the lights back on, but faced with a late-night commute.

In a two-decade consulting career I have pulled all sorts of late night firefighting, client hand-holding gigs. It comes with many of the jobs we choose to do. Often it will bring you closer to your clients, make you a much better consultant and enhance your reputation.

Getting a buzz on holiday

Early in my independent consulting career (and the only time it has ever happened), I was tracked down on holiday in France by a client in New York. They had a critical problem that for some reason they thought required my assistance. I left my family and flew to the USA one day, met the client on the second day and flew back that evening, landing early the following morning. I was back basking on the beach in Normandy at midday. Maybe I am unusual, but I got a huge kick out of that. Possibly because the only way to get there and back was on Concorde. There was a buzz about the whole thing; someone truly valued my advice. Instead of being a bad experience, it was a milestone in my career as an independent – I'd arrived!

Set the pattern for YOUR work ethic

But you do need to know why you are doing it. Back to that plan of yours that needs constant updating and revision. Part of that is getting clients to understand how *you* work. In this, behaviour patterns are vital. Clients can and do use and abuse independent consultants fairly brutally at times. So you need to set some rules that – without being articulated too directly – are very, very clear. If you are seen as ready to drop everything and change plans just because they need to see you, they will feed on this insecurity. Never, ever let that happen. Very often in my own experience it is as simple as taking your client aside and explaining that you do have other commitments. While stating that you do value their business, they also have to understand that you are not 'employed' exclusively by them.

Now I know that when you are scratching around like a chicken in a yard for business that can seem hard to do, but it is good advice. Give in too early and when you look back later you will regret it. When there's little business in the offing, it is easy to say 'Yes, yes, yes' to anything. Unless you are about to go out of business and put a huge stain on the family escutcheon, don't do it. You *will* regret it later.

Of course, just about anyone who has stayed the course for two decades has grabbed at one of those tempting offers, when business has been in the doldrums: I admit, I have done it myself. Did I regret it? Yes! Did I do anything about it? Oh yes. As soon as we were back in funds I fired the client. There is nothing more satisfying than firing a client – it produces a golden glow inside that lasts for quite a time.

These are the times that no one (until now) ever tells you about. The dark days when you need a certain resilience to keep going. Virtually everyone I know has had these, and you need a great deal of confidence and self-belief to stay optimistic. You may recall, I described earlier that you need shoulders to cry on sometimes – these are those times.

There will be – almost have to be – times when you will work on projects you don't like and don't believe in for the very basic reason that there isn't much else you can do. Anyone – including those in the big firms – who tells you different is being at the very least economical with the truth. It is the independent's version of, in corporate life, getting a new boss and discovering mutual hatred. The only outcome is to knuckle down and get on with it, and then get out as swiftly and cleanly as you can.

The upside – yes, there is always an upside – is that you will have learned a lot. And that sort of experience is, if you want to take a positive approach, extremely valuable in making you better able to survive in the future.

Missing your mates, and cabin fever

To compound the trauma of going it alone are the twin terrors of missing your mates and cabin fever. It isn't until you actually sit in that chair in your new 'office' for a week that it really dawns on you what you have done. Days can be long. Depending on the kind of consulting you are doing, there can be long periods when you are – literally – working on your own. Certainly most of us spend time outside our self-created cabinet of horrors, but it takes a good three to six months to begin to get the hang of really being alone.

Over the years, those making the transition from employee to solo worker have listed these as some of the major things they miss about not being surrounded by other co-workers:

Loss of office social life. Few of us realise until it is too late that the sandwich around the corner, the coffee or glass of wine after work are key parts of the day. The answer to this is to look around where you are working now and see if you can find alternatives. Chances are, that unless you are in the Hebrides, living in a Norwegian fjord or up a Swiss Alp, there is a like-minded person pretty close by.

Loss of colleagues' expertise. This can be really tough. The interaction we have come to take for granted is suddenly not there. My advice is to try and stay in touch with some of your old colleagues, or create a support network that you can call to talk and try out ideas.

Feeling 'trapped' at home 24 hours a day. Where consultants have major projects, this kind of cabin fever can assume serious levels. Like anything else, you have to learn to recognise it and destroy it. Make a point of just taking a walk – even for 15 minutes in the morning and afternoon. I take the dog out, and also talk to it for most of the time if I am cooped up. I am a great believer in dogs and cats in the solo workers' environment.

Reduced training opportunities. You never miss it until it isn't there. Now staying ahead and up-to-speed is all about personal responsibility and personal cost. Danger is, if you don't invest in your own knowledge, you'll become out of touch very fast.

Reduced equipment facilities. When you had that 'job', you had all the hardware and software you would ever need – and you never appreciated it. Now you are responsible for that all by yourself. Clients move rapidly up the software curve, and you need to do the same. It is very embarrassing to be unable to download because you haven't got the latest update.

Poor working facilities. Face it, MegaCorps' offices were pretty cool, weren't they? That noodle bar and Starbucks in reception, and the free magazines, games and DVDs, were to die for. Now, it is all on you. So, make your new work environment is the very best you can make it (see Chapter 3).

Reduced information input. Like lack of colleagues' expertise and being cut off from training, you just don't get the information that keeps you up-to-date anymore. So seek out new ways. Take a coffee break and surf the Internet. Create a list of favourite places that will keep you going. Subscribe to magazines, go to shows, and network and keep in touch with those colleagues.

The partner and the kids

We may have touched on this before, but when you really begin to work from home, those rules I talked about earlier can go quickly out of the window. This is especially true if cabin fever does set in, or you miss someone to talk to. It is all too easy to sneak into the kitchen for a cup of coffee and a little dialogue. But you can't give into that. Call your 'shoulder-to-cry-on' mates by all means, but stick it out. You have to establish not just in your mind, but in the minds of everyone else, that what you are doing is paramount (worried already?).

Looking back over the years, I realise that for most of my solo-work friends and their partners had little understanding of what they did, and frankly didn't show much more than the most passing interest. The fact that you will possibly be worried about how going independent is going to turn out will tend to make you irritable and short tempered too! So, hopefully, they will spend a large part of the day avoiding you as much as possible. It may be at this time that you wished you'd taken that little shared office on the High Street, even if it was over your budget. Indeed, finding out what you actually do can come as something of a shock for partners, especially if you are taking over parts of the home you share. I know we all hear about couples who are totally compatible and are going to create a great business together. Well, in my experience those are created by Hollywood scriptwriters, and have no bearing on cold reality.

I knew a very austere, precise Scandinavian consultant who described this discovery process as 'the moment that the home becomes a machine for working in, when the norms and expectations for social life at home are challenged'. He went on to say that, 'At this point it does seem necessary to establish an etiquette for working within the domestic scene, regarding the division between work and leisure.' I call this a sensible, diplomatic Norwegian way of saying, 'Stay out of my space until six o'clock or else.'

What you need to realise as a home worker is that what you are doing is just as much a strange alien experience for the rest of the family. If you have children, they will find it difficult to realise that Daddy or Mummy is home all day. Moreover, they will find it difficult to accept that you are actually working. Be prepared for that, it's going to happen. As I said in Chapter 1, set rules early and stick with them. But expect to see some disruption too. This isn't just a new experience for you: it is a new adventure for everyone around you.

The social v business thing

There seem to be very few independent consultants who are totally able to separate their professional and private lives (that's why a lot of people find it impossible, and prefer the black-and-white lifestyle that a nine to five job offers). This is particularly exacerbated when you work from home.

The important thing is making sure that you are able to switch off and have a private life. What you need to be able to do is set rules so you don't find yourself at the beck and call of clients at all hours of the day and night.

Let's hang out at your place

I had a client who was giving me a lot of business, but always seemed to end up at my office at the end of a working day. I was living in another apartment, and he seemed always to end up having a drink or dinner. Turned out that he was going through the first part of what eventually ended in a break-up of his marriage. I was the convenient place to hang out. My solution (probably the cowardly one) was to explain that I wasn't going to be 'home' and then agree to meet him somewhere other than my office, where I could usually 'park' him with someone else.

Admittedly, when you are trying to build up a business, it is difficult to turn people away: but some times you just need to, for your own – and possibly your family's – sanity. That is why I advocate – if you work from home – having a separate entrance from the outside into your workspace (see Chapter 3), even if it means knocking a hole in the wall to accommodate a new door. Not only is this a more professional solution, but it stops getting family and business mixed up.

But today, it is practically impossible to have real separation barriers between your work and your play time. If you are working in a specific community (as a local accountant for example), your business life and social life will naturally run in parallel for much of the time.

Equally, if you are another sort of professional (personal trainer, business consultant) you will probably need to spend 'investment' time with clients, which is a social activity. Indeed, throughout my time as an independent consultant, many of my clients have come through a social meeting. And the more people that take up solo working as a means to earn a living, the more the social and professional lines will blur.

Looking at it from another angle, most of the people you will end up working with as a solo operator will be people you like, trust and whose professional skills you admire. This is one of the great advantages of working for yourself. You get to choose your co-workers. Clients can be a different thing entirely! But even there, the ones you don't really like rarely last. Subconsciously, we all seem able to move on from the people we don't enjoy working with. If you look back on your own career, you will quickly see what I mean.

Taking time off

When you start up an independent business, it is hard to begin thinking of time off. Your purpose in life is to get established and create a viable operation that can support you and whoever else is part of your life. All of us have had those moments when we say, 'I just can't afford to go away, what happens if …'. Well, a very old friend of mine changed my mind on this, by applying a piece of very subtle psychology.

'Just imagine,' he said, 'that you had to go to the USA for some meetings. You'd take a week out, wouldn't you?' Well, you don't need to lie to your clients if you want to take a week off, just say that you are going travelling.'

And from that day on, that's what I have done. At the beginning of each year, I ink out the weeks when I am 'travelling'. Believe me, it works. There might be a time every so often when something destroys the plan: but basically, if you tell people you are going to be away that week it is accepted. The uncool way to do it is the Friday morning before you depart. Then there will *always* be an emergency. Once clients understand that you are not there 365 days a year, they will quickly 'get' it.

Tip! If you don't travel much for work there are always training weeks, professional conferences and other reasons for 'travelling'.

And you do need to get away. Breaks are good for the soul. Although I refer to being in touch on the road in more detail in Chapter 3, when you go 'travelling' make sure people can get in touch with you easily. When I am on holiday I always have my mobile phone, and usually a laptop as well. And it is always useful to know the location of the nearest Internet café (even if you have no plans to use it). These days I use a professional answering service when I go into holiday mode. For a small fee I get my calls to the office diverted, seamlessly, and a voice answers using my company name. Then they give me by e-mail, fax or phone a list of the calls. If it is a period of intense activity, I will call in once a day. But if my answering service knows how to reach me,

Tip! When going on holiday, call the hotel in advance and see if you can get Internet access at the location. It saves you carrying a laptop with you. Equally, if you are using a villa or apartment, ask the rental company what facilities they have, and if there are any known 'dead zones' (where mobile phone reception is poor or non-existent).

I rarely call in more than once a week. Let's face it, if something really does blow up, all your clients *should* know your mobile number.

Playing the percentage game

Individuals contemplating a leap into the unknown world of the independent often ask me how much of their time should be spent on new business development. I think the answer to that is another of life's great mysteries. It depends entirely on the type of consulting you are going to do, and the variety and intensity of the work. Some consultants I know never have to go looking for business: it just comes in. Neither do they ever have to market themselves – all their business comes from world of mouth.

That said, unless you are very, very lucky (even if you are very, very good), there are going to be times when business goes a little slack. At that point it is too late. What you need to do is spend a certain percentage of your work time looking for future work. In my case, for example, while I have some regular assignments, few go on forever (circumstances and people change too much for that). Also, in my case much of the work I do is based on a project that has a distinct beginning, middle and end. While you may be able to prolong the end, because there is often some unplanned activity that wasn't in the initial brief, there is usually a sense of finality. At that point you need to have that pipeline primed for more business.

Now I know it is difficult when you are busy to stop and begin looking for the next business, but you have to. All successful independent consultants do this rigorously and with a regularity that would probably surprise those who have never been in this position.

Taking a five-day week as a norm, I would suggest that to maintain a proper flow of business in normal economic times, you need to spend 20 per cent of your time on new business development. Now if you are sitting fat and sassy and up to your ears in business, you are probably shaking your head, thinking, 'No, no, no, I don't need this.'

There is a very simple answer to that: YES YOU DO!

I don't know anyone who has ever survived past that 24-month watershed without assiduously prospecting for business. Just as employees get made redundant, so independent consultants get similar treatment.

So, 20 per cent in good times (that works out to roughly one day a week), and up to 40 per cent at other times. You'll soon learn how to judge what you've got in the pipeline, remembering that just because you write a proposal doesn't mean that it will naturally translate into work.

> *The one-third, one-third, one-third model*
>
> Sometimes a good dose of cynicism keep us independents alive. One solo worker suggests (and this can, I'll agree, be true at some times in our consultant lives) that the more accurate breakdown for any independent today is one-third, one-third, one-third. This she explains as one-third of your time to get business; one-third of the time to carry out the assignment; and the final one-third trying to get paid by the client. Don't laugh, it's serious and you would do well to reflect on the fact that this is what can happen: you need to be ready for it.

Business development covers many types of activity. It can include networking, events, visits to clients and prospects, marketing activity through mail or the Internet, and so forth. It could be writing articles, giving speeches and making yourself as visible as possible (Chapter 5 covers this in detail). It can be taking the right contact out for lunch or a drink.

But do it. And have a plan for it. Many of us, certainly in the early years as we struggle to get established and develop a reputation, do much of this activity out of mainstream business hours or at weekends. But one thing I advise that will help you to get a true picture of your working week is …

Keep time sheets

In a lot of professions, time sheets are the way of accounting for the time we spend on a client's business. But what I am advocating here is to keep a rolling time sheet on everything you do in the business. Log all the calls and e-mails you make or receive. Log the time you work on client business, and the time you take off for 'thinking' time or a coffee/sandwich break. Log all the time you are idle as well – you'll be quite surprised how much of that there really is.

If you do that for a month, you'll begin to build up an honest – well, it will be honest if you are honest with yourself – picture of your overall activity. My bet is that you will probably astound yourself just how much time you waste. I had a work colleague who discovered that he was wasting about one day in five. So he replanned his business day and took the time off!

Tip! Put the time sheet onto an Excel spreadsheet and just open it up every day. That way you can simply click and record. You can also get into the ritual of tidying it up every night before you log off.

By doing this, you will begin to 'understand' what you do, and how, possibly, you can improve. It is the one way of getting a true look at your activities.

Never put all your beans in one tin

This may be the post-modern version of eggs in a basket, but it sounds a little more contemporary. My point here (and we hark back to that advice above about how much time should you spend on business development) is that I have seen too many independents (and even those with three, or four, or more employees) getting it terribly wrong by putting virtually all their business with one client. Note what I have said – 'virtually all *their* business'. The client rarely knows that you have – in reality – bet the farm on his future. *You* do.

It is so, so, so easy to go down this route. You start work, you get a really good client, they give you more and more work. You even think that the work has diversified, because you are now working for this group and that group, Division A and Division B and so on. Wake up! You are not. You are working for the *same* company. You may actually have done what we talked about and primed that new business pump. And where better to do it than somewhere you can get easy access to others, who feel comfortable with you, because you already work with their colleagues? But this is *not* business development. This is business evolvement (which we will talk about in the next chapter).

Today's business world is a cruel, fast-changing and unforgiving place. And it doesn't matter where or how you work: as that famous phrase has it – shit happens. Yes it does. And if we have all our beans piled up in one tin, they are going to get burned – badly.

The following two stories explain why evolving your business inside one firm is *not* a good idea.

- Two work colleagues set up together. They quickly landed a dream client: a large, expanding international corporation. As the client grew, so did they, taking on people, expanding their offices. Although they had other business, these other clients took second place. Within three years, more than 90 per cent of all their business came from the one major client (albeit split across industries, divisions and geographies). Then one day, the whole dream turned into a nightmare. The company they had toiled so loyally for was bought in a surprise acquisition. Within six months they had no business – it had all devolved to the new owner's own in-house and external support.
- A highly successful marketing consulting firm (of three partners) became the de facto in-house cross-border marketing team for a large US multi-national's operations in Europe. Gradually, they became virtually the only

client. One day, the president, who had championed this small creative group, left the business. The new incumbent – by nature a cost-cutter – issued a series of edicts within 48 hours of getting into the job. One of these was 'No external consultants, under any circumstances.' The rest, as they say, is not a nice story.

Advice: You can't predict the future. We are all vulnerable. As independents, it is those times when we feel the most secure that we are in fact the most vulnerable, because we have probably reached the zenith of that relationship. Prime the pump – develop, develop, develop.

This type of situation is typical. And it doesn't matter whether you are working in a local, national or international market context. Things change:

- The bottom, literally, falls out of a market. Everyone in that industry is having a really bad time. You are no longer a solution, you are a cost. Advice: Try, wherever possible, to work across a range of industries. Usually, they don't all take a dive together.
- Mergers and acquisitions can quickly and seriously affect your small business.
- Changes of management. The CEO or the CFO you have so assiduously developed over the years is suddenly gone. It is time to start all over again.

So, watch carefully. Nothing in this business is for ever, no matter how good it looks today on how good you are.

Stay fit

With all this worry about getting a business off the ground, and then, when it is finally running like a well-oiled machine, about whether it will all implode, it is amazing that we aren't all thin, twitching wrecks. Thing is, if you haven't got some resilience you won't start life as a consultant in the first place. But luckily, it isn't all doom and gloom. Certainly, there will be some low points, but we have just got to make the best of them and move on.

However, being fit adds a great deal to that resilience. The one thing an independent consultant can't afford is to have a serious illness. The theory of an 'ounce of prevention' was never truer than in this profession. Remember, you are all you've got. There is just you and your intellectual property. No one can use that on your behalf. So what is your unique offering is also your Achilles' heel. Unlike a shopkeeper or a manufacturer, people can't sell the stock of your business – you – unless you are there. Therefore, taking care of yourself is of paramount importance.

First you need to stay fit. I have a longstanding colleague who says that he makes a point – whatever is happening – of having two good sessions at the gym each week. Me, I walk the dog – often long distances. It doesn't matter what you do, but you need to make sure you are able to get up and go (especially as you may find that in your new role you spend more hours sitting than you did as an employee).

Related to the need to get physical exercise is watching what you eat. It is all too easy – especially if your office is part of the family home – to snack from the fridge or sabotage the biscuit supply. Don't.

Try to get the kind of diet that makes it easy for you to work. I am not a dietician or a nutritionist – as those who know me will most certainly testify! – but I do try and eat as healthy as I can. You need to be able to work long and hard at times, to travel and to meet people. So mobility and the ability to think clearly for long periods are vital.

My view is that part of the pacing yourself that I talked about above is all about taking breaks. So many of us these days spend a large part of our lives at a workstation staring at a VDU: we do need to get up a stretch every so often. Those exercises that long-haul airline operators now advise you do on their flights are the kind of thing I mean. If you are not up for that, then just getting up every hour or so and crossing the room to put the kettle on, or a similar activity, can stop you staying locked in one position for too long.

Health checks

Whatever your age, make sure you consult your doctor on a regular basis – and your dentist. If you need to have things done, get them done. Otherwise they always happen when you are at your busiest. Also, I have never seen a successful independent consultant with bad teeth! Think about it.

Health and work insurance

Your time is precious. That, after all, is all you have. So get good health insurance that covers you wherever you may be. It won't be cheap, but get it anyway. It should cover you 365 days a year, wherever you may be, and your travel as well. My own experience is that if it looks really cheap the service and the result will be too. If nothing else it will give you peace of mind. Also, I advise a professional insurance that will pay out if you lose the ability to work. Consider how much you need to live comfortably, and then insure yourself for that. Again it won't be cheap, but it will provide a security net if something really bad happens.

> ### To hell and back
>
> I know what it is like to suddenly find yourself unable to work effectively. A few years ago, I slipped two discs in my back. I was confined to bed for six weeks! Once they got the basic pain under control I was OK, except for the fact that I couldn't move. However, I was able to get hold of a specially angled tray that held my laptop, so I could lie horizontal and work happily (it is more fun that watching daytime TV), using e-mail and the phone. Luckily I had some understanding clients. I was even able to use the time to reflect on next-step strategies. So, even when times look grim, if you search around you'll find some sort of silver lining.

Saving for the future

Yes, you need to do it, but the options are endless. My advice is to talk to your accountant, banker or independent financial adviser. Also, get a second opinion – too many of them have proved wrong these last years. Whatever you do, don't put all those beans in the same tin.

Finding and dealing with suppliers

Good suppliers can, and often do, determine just how successful you will be. Rule one is very straightforward. For professional advice (financial, legal and IT), get the best that you can decently afford. If you go and see an accountant who immediately tells you how much he is going to save you and how much tax you won't have to pay – leave.

You DO need a good **accountant**. I have never found good accountants any more expensive than bad ones. If you find yours is bad, fire him quick. It may seem like a pain, but it will pay off later.

You MAY need a good **law firm**. Not because you expect to get sued, but just to get quick, friendly – and timely – advice. The time to appoint a good law firm is when you don't need it. Also, it is a good place to have arranged for filing papers of incorporation of the business, getting official papers notarised and so forth.

A **bank** is going to be a must-have. My advice is choose the one in your area that has the best total services (and that includes a manager over the age of 35!). Go for one initially that will open free business accounts and give you lots of free services. Keep your personal life and your professional life well apart. That means get a business account, with a cash and credit card. Also, I would advise getting a card that offers virtually unlimited credit if you need it, and one that also gives you lots of points/airmiles. Get to know the manager, and see if you can run a line of credit if really required. If you are doing international business, see what they offer between Euro, Sterling, Swiss franc and US dollar accounts.

In these technologically-driven days, you need a good **IT adviser**. Who you appoint depends on your business and how much you know and can handle confidently yourself. If you are small, get someone who is also small, but has some leverage when it comes to building and buying the equipment (hardware and software) that you need. Most important: they need to be close by. If you have a mega-virus feasting on your hard drive, you need someone who can be there quick.

Equally, unless you are very good at this sort of thing yourself, get a **webmaster** who can make sure that your website stays up-to-date. I know a lot of older independent consultants who have clearly failed to embrace the coming of the digital age. Not having a website is one sign of this. Frankly I doubt that I will ever get much business from having a well-maintained site. But what it does is explain who I am and what I do. Its main function for my business is to allow people to check me out. Particularly when I am doing research, I find that while I am on the phone, people are on-line checking up on who I am and how legitimate my business really is. My view? Websites are increasingly important. They are the company brochure of the twenty-first century (except a lot cheaper to produce and update).

> *Tip! Get a monthly account with your local taxi firm. It means you can get around town, to railways stations and airports without having to think about cash. They are also useful for picking up clients and ferrying documents around as required.*

Depending on your business, there are many other suppliers that could be critical, for example, **printers, transport firms, couriers, travel agents, leasing firms, insurance brokers.** In all cases, ask around, find who uses different organisations and why.

Where do letterheads, pencils and printer ink come from?

Sorry, you'll have to go to Chapter 3 for the answer to this. But, in start-up mode, think carefully. I doubt you need anything like as much as you think you do.

Cars, personal and corporate taxation, buying v leasing equipment

You'll find details of all these in Chapter 6.

Insurance

Make sure that your office (even if it is part of your home) is adequately insured, and that any equipment that you regularly travel with (phones, laptops, cameras) is fully covered. Do shop around: rates very hugely, and from year to year. Advice: some insurance firms frown on home offices, and will certainly demand that they are separately insured – otherwise the house and content insurance can be null and void if something happens. Make sure that you are adequately protected.

In Chapter 3, we are going to look at how you should go about setting up your workplace.

Key learning points

- Find out if you can get your present employer to 'fund' your transition to an independent by offering guaranteed (or even ad hoc) work.
- If you do a deal, make sure you have a legal document or contract that lays out the terms and conditions.
- Take out the daily commute and work from or close to home, which gives you 10 to 15 hours a week extra to work on your new business.
- It really helps to have a long-term plan so you have goals to shoot for.
- Almost anyone can be a consultant. Today more and more people are taking the plunge: yacht designers, sports medicine practitioners, events managers and the rest.
- For some – coming up to enforced retirement – independent consulting is the twenty-first century equivalent of the safety of the garden shed.
- You MUST find ways to get that administration done – don't leave it. If you can afford it, get someone to help you.
- If you get busy and are out of the office a lot, a 'helper' makes sense too.
- Bank direct debits save getting cut off from vital services (eg phone and electric) if you travel a lot.
- Save time: pile up all your payments and do them once a month.
- Same goes for invoicing: don't forget to get it out on time or you won't get paid.
- Always get at least one-third of the project budget up front.
- Have a production plan as a guide to current business and future opportunities, and update it weekly.
- Learn to pace your day – don't become a workaholic. Get out, take a walk, exercise.

- Everyone has down days. Don't sit and mope about – go treat yourself to a coffee or 'sneak' off to lunch, you'll feel better.
- Don't abandon important personal milestones or family obligations to fight fires – you'll regret it later if you do.
- Learn how to take time off.
- Don't forget you need that shoulder to cry on.
- Feeling trapped at home and getting cabin fever are normal. Just learn to get out and do other things.
- Remember to set rules on your workspace so you are not interrupted.
- Never forget to prime the pump – spend 20 per cent of work time on business development.
- No matter how enticing it looks, never, ever work for only one client – it is long-term suicide.
- Find good suppliers: accountant, law firm, bank, IT support and a web-master if you can't do it yourself.
- Get insured – you know it makes sense.

Chapter 3

Creating YOUR workplace

My husband said he needed more space, so I locked him outside.

Roseanne Barr

YOUR workplace. Doesn't that sound good? For some peculiar reason it's not at all like going to THEIR workplace, where, if you are lucky – in these days of open-plan, hot-desking, drop in 'work pods' – you may have the ultimate luxury: your own desk. This is your place. And while it certainly needs to have your personality stamped on it, my view is that this grows with time.

Since I began my independent consultant's career in 1982, I've had a total of five different offices. While I may have had the basic idea of what I needed (see below), after a few months they sort of settled down and developed into a really personal space. Basically, what happened was that they became comfortable like an old shoe. They may have developed a few cracks and lost their shine, but you felt at home there.

So as you begin to consider life as a solo operator, you need to spend some time thinking through what this 'space' has to achieve if it is to be effective.

Also remember that for many independents a large part of their working life may well be spent on the road, meeting customers and working at client locations. While I am yet to be convinced that you can work efficiently in the so-called 'virtual office' where your workspace is anywhere there is a wireless LAN, the overall physical 'footprint' we require has certainly shrunk. However, consider this: if you are the kind of consultant (like myself) who spends weeks out of an office, but then comes back to toil away on projects, just how much space do you need, and what facilities need to

Tip! What you need is somewhere that is efficient and yet makes you feel good. When you have to sit there on a sunny Sunday morning, because a client (who you just know is off playing golf) needs something for Monday at nine o'clock, then you had better have a workplace that attracts you.

be there? This is going to be your 'home' for up to twelve hours a day. You need to like it.

As I said earlier, for post-industrial man, the independent's workspace becomes the equivalent of the garden shed or greenhouse. To tell the truth, I often 'escape' to my workspace, because it provides a haven when others areas of the house suddenly develop into 'no-go' zones. It is also where I keep track of my personal life outside of direct work. So paying bills, leisure Internet surfing and shopping and family travel planning all take place in my space. It is convenient and it works for me. Whether this kind of arrangement works for you is a matter of temperament and personal circumstances.

To get you thinking seriously about the workspace issue, I have created a short questionnaire, which should help you reach some basic conclusions about wants and needs. Getting an early understanding of what your working requirements are going to be helps save costly mistakes and corrections later. But remember, as I keep saying, you don't have to have it all right away. Just try and make sure that you create a space that can expand over time. After the questionnaire, I have repeated the questions and added a commentary based on my own experiences.

Can I work from home?   ☐ yes ☐ no

Can I have a dedicated area in my home?   ☐ yes ☐ no

Will I have clients visiting my home?   ☐ yes ☐ no

Will I principally work:
    from my home office?   ☐ yes ☐ no

    on the road (hotels etc.)   ☐ yes ☐ no

    at my client's premises?   ☐ yes ☐ no

Can I create an external access to my home office?   ☐ yes ☐ no

Do I have enough room to expand, store files and add
    equipment as the business grows?   ☐ yes ☐ no

Do I have room to create a stand-alone office unit?   ☐ yes ☐ no

Do I have room to expand that facility if I need to at a
    later date?   ☐ yes ☐ no

Are there alternative facilities in my town/near my location
    I can use?   ☐ yes ☐ no

Can I share offices and costs with other professionals?   ☐ yes ☐ no

Will I require planning permission to create my office?   ☐ yes ☐ no

Hopefully, from answering the questionnaire, you now have a clear idea of what is easy to do, what will take some time (and funds), and what you should leave well alone until you get the business established (by which time it may be sensible to consider moving anyway).

Now let's backtrack and look at these very basic issues again, adding the light of experience.

Basic issues

Can I work from home?

I know we have touched on this in earlier chapters, but this is the big decision. If you have any doubts that you will find it impossible (because of young children, elderly relatives, noisy environment) then you do need to seek out an alternative. If you simply don't have the space to create your own secure work area, the same applies. Here's a great test: your best client is on the phone and you are having a four-way conference call that will last an hour. Are you certain you can put aside that time, take notes and contribute fully in the workspace you are considering you will occupy? Is the dog going to bark at the postman? Is your six-month-old daughter going to wake up for her feed? These are the distractions you can't afford to have as a busy, committed professional. For anyone contemplating life as a solo operator, this is THE big decision (well, the big decision after deciding that you are going to give this life a try).

Can I have a dedicated area in my home?

If you've solved problem one and decided you CAN work from home (possibly because you are single or your partner goes to a 'real' job every day), the next step is to decide where you are going to work. Clearly, wherever you work it has to be secure in one way or another. Also, if you are working from the house or apartment, it has to be somewhere where you can leave things and go about the rest of your life. It isn't much fun (after the first flush of being independent has worn off) having to move your entire 'office' because you have friends coming to stay. Similarly, if you have a partner who works nine to five, five days a week, he or she will have to get used to your fledgling independent operator's need to catch up or prepare on weekends. In my time, I have seen some ingenious mini-workspaces (that make a lot of sense when you are starting out), but they all could be secured and locked away. Face it, you don't want your friends and relations going through your work, or just 'borrowing' a pencil, do you?

Will I have clients visiting my home?

My view: if you can keep clients away from your house, do so. If you haven't got some external access or external office (see below), it seems that no time is ever a good time. If they are simply checking you out and you can't avoid it, get it over with quick and then take them to lunch or something. Many of my clients are friends and over the years we have been to each others houses (for dinner and so on), but that is a more social affair. That's fine, but if you have restricted work conditions don't try and do business across the kitchen table while the dog chews the client's shoes and the kids spill juice all over him.

Can I create an external access to my home office?

If you want to work from home and want a secure space to do it in, think about creating a space that has access from outside, so clients and suppliers can come and go without disturbing or being aware of the rest of the activity in the house. I have several work colleagues who have done this in a variety of ways:

- An IT consultant reconfigured his original garage (built into the house) and turned it into an office space, with a front door from the driveway. It also retained the access door into the rest of the house. He plumbed in a small toilet, so that visiting clients (in his case he had quite a few) didn't have to invade the house at all.
- An independent website creator found an apartment with a maid's room (and toilet) attached that had external access to the main staircase. It was small but it provided a great place to start for a small additional rental.
- A young independent marketing communications consultant (his words), otherwise known as a freelance copywriter (my words), turned the base-ment of the house he rents (well, he rents one floor) into a wonderful workspace (excellent for those who don't care about natural light!). Again, the big upside was that it had direct access from the main corridor, making it fully independent from the living quarters.

As with any of these alternatives to 'real' offices, they need to be presentable. While it would perhaps be nice to think that all our clients were as off-the-wall as we are, this is rarely true. So, without being too conservative, make your offices your own, and – as I emphasised above – try not to invite the clients over.

Do I have room to create a stand-alone office unit?

When you have some more space available, you are only limited by the level of your imagination; and having a sanctuary where you can work undis-turbed is a great boost to any budding independent career. However convenient and cheap working from inside the four walls of the family home may be, there is nothing to beat being able to have the freedom that some type of stand-alone unit can bring.

Today, recognising the increasing trend for people to work from their home base, manufacturers are coming up with all sorts of shapes, sizes and styles of office for the home worker. While many appear to be little more than one small evolutionary step from the ubiquitous garden shed, others are system-built to meet the needs of the twenty-first-century solo operator.

If you do go down the 'office in the garden' type of route, here are a few things to consider.

- What will the neighbours say? People can be funny (particularly if your cat has a tendency to eat their goldfish), so it is a good idea (even if you don't need their permission) to tell them what you are about to do.
- Get a lot of quotes. And check out local suppliers (I've found them often cheaper than the ones you see in the home and garden magazines). If you want ideas of types and prices try out www.hutdesign.co.uk, www.createspace.com and www.aarco.co.uk. All have home offices for the garden or external space that range in price from around £5,000 (self-assembly[7]) to over £15,000. If you want something really special (think expensive) try www.oakmasters.co.uk, www.romseyfarm.fsnet.co.uk or www.oakframedirectory.co.uk.
- Get everything you can plumbed, wired and piped in. It is important to get the specification agreed early on – you don't want to have to tear up the floorboards after six months.
- Get twice as many electrical sockets as you think you'll need (or count all those you KNOW you will need and multiply by two!).
- Be careful with the positioning of the office. You don't want to miss out on sunlight, but neither do you want it to blind you or make your screen unreadable.
- Good lighting is vital, but so is light from windows. Think skylight (with blinds you can lower!). You also need a few external lights, so you don't fall down on the way home across the garden.
- You need ventilation, so make sure windows open easily.
- You need to heat and COOL most garden offices. The solution is to get an all-purpose air conditioner that will maintain a basic level of temperature all year round. There are wall-mounted domestic units from Samsung,

---

[7] Unless you are the DIY king of independent consultants, don't try and do this yourself. Get a professional and pay them to do it properly. This IS a tool of your trade: make sure it works to the full. Anyway, while you are trying to construct the damn thing you are not doing your business.

Panasonic, Fujitsu and Toshiba, among others, that range in price from around £1,500 to £2,000 installed. Go to their websites and check them out. BUT, if you are going to buy, two tips! Get one that is professionally installed and has a service contract deal with it; and make sure it is installed when you put up the construction.

- Put in a toilet facility and hot and cold water (there are plenty of small water heaters that work well). You don't want the disturbance of running across to the house every time nature calls!
- Install a fridge, a kettle and a microwave. This will keep you fully functional and focused on the task in hand. I also have a nice big couch, great for reading on, which pulls out as a bed. It is also great if you find yourself in the dog house (or late getting back from a night out with your pals!), or for those rare times when the entire family comes to stay.
- When it comes to furniture, well, there's always Ikea! Seriously, there is nothing wrong with their products for small offices. The other idea is a bespoke office build. Be careful here. I priced out several of these office creators (who advertise in the Sunday newspapers and home magazines) and found them around 50 per cent more than my local carpenter.
- Don't forget maintenance. There is no point in waiting until something goes wrong. Keep it maintained – the painting, guttering and wood proofing – and regularly check the wiring, heaters etc. And make sure you have an annually maintained fire extinguisher.
- Finally, security. Does it have decent locks on doors and windows and is it all insured?

Of course, you don't have to build one of these as a stand-alone: you can always add-on. Lots of people I know have added to the rear of or built on top of garages, or converted existing outbuildings. The importance thing is to have a good plan about what you want to do and get that budget set. Unless you are really short of funds, try and get all the basics built in at the time of any conversion.

Do I have room to expand that facility?

When you begin your own consulting firm, it is unlikely you will know where you will be in five years' time, let alone ten. So, where possible, consider carefully the size and accessibility of the office set-up. For example, if you were to have co-workers, would there be room for them or would you have to either build anew or consider renting offices elsewhere? Remember, you don't have to fill all the space, just know that it is there if you need to expand.

Recently, I had an assignment that involved three other key players. Because I had created a sizeable home office I was able to accommodate all of them in my rural 'war room', without having to squeeze. While this might never happen to you, it is useful to have the space for later expansion or as an 'extra' feature when you sell on.

The other thing about space is that it really does fill up. You are going to create files (that you legally need to keep) and you probably (depending on your business) require storage for publications and an inventory of the published materials you use in your business. This all takes up room. In addition, you might add office equipment. A colleague of mine got into terrible trouble when he found himself with an all-singing, all-dancing state-of-the-art copying machine. To accommodate it (he needed to make a large number of complex documents) he had to entirely re-design his office. If his space had been just a little larger, none of that would have happened.

Are there alternative facilities in my town I can use?

If finding space and working from your own location just isn't going to work, or you simply just need others around you, then finding a location you can operate from should not be that difficult. These days, even the smallest town – and some villages too – seem to have all sorts of options (it seems that half the farmers in England are turning disused cow sheds into office accommodation!). Obviously what you rent or buy is going to depend on the type of business you are starting and the kind of budget you have. But to start with, think about what you need and what facilities will be required (see our workspace in the garden checklist above). Light and ventilation, and plumbed and wired-in services are all important.

Tip! When I have intensive work sessions with others at my workplace in the garden I never let them stay at the house. Reason? If you are putting in 10 or 12 hours of time together (and usually for four or five days at a time) everyone appreciates down-time. It is also unfair on your spouse and children. What I do is book them into the local public house (200 metres away, with en suite rooms and a killer breakfast!) so they have their own space. I am not being unfriendly (often I'll go and have a drink or dinner with them at the end of the day), but when I suggest this arrangement, everyone I've worked with likes it better.

If you have to meet with clients, is there a meeting room you can reserve? Will your commute be easy; can you park the car? It is getting the answers to the basics that will determine how useful your new workspace will be.

Can I share offices and costs with other professionals?

If you are looking for this type of solution, the next step is to consider whether you can 'bunk-up' with some like minded independents. This has a lot of advantages. Often there are shared services, everything from IT to a kitchen to an answering service. In addition to the advantage of being able to share costs, I know quite a few professionals who have found the 'social' atmosphere alone a compelling reason to continue like this. They say that being able to share ideas, as well as high and lows, with others is a huge advantage. Others just need to be out of the home environment in their professional life.

If you decide to go down this route, it is really important to get the deal in writing, so you know just what you are buying into. Failure to do that can result in all sorts of hidden charges and costs. And it is not only important to know the costs on your way in. You need to be fully aware of what it will cost to get out, too.

Will I require planning permission to create my office?

There are not many places these days where you can just build what you like. And while most constructors and builders will try and suggest that a small office doesn't need planning permission from the local authorities, don't bet on it. It all depends on where you are located and local regulations. What you need to do is pre-empt any action by checking it out BEFORE you go ahead. Having to file for permission retroactively can be costly and time-consuming (neither of which you need). My view: know where you are before you start.

Fixing up the facilities

I explained above in the checklist for creating an external office that you need a few must-haves like air-conditioning and good lighting. This is just as true for an office inside your home. What you want is a pleasant working environment that lets you perform to the very best. So check them out, you will be glad you did.

Play safe

Go out and buy a safe. Crazy? OK, you haven't got the Queen's Crown Jewels in your office, but you've got something more important – your life. Lose all that and where would you be? A decent safe is not that expensive. You can buy one that will store what I have listed below for less than £300 (€450) and one of those hotel type digi-safes (that you can have cemented or cut into the wall in a discreet place for under £150 (€200). That's a small price to pay for peace of mind.

What you need is one that is (a) fireproof and (b) heavy enough to give two burglars a guaranteed hernia trying to lift it. My safe (I've had it for 20 years) contains:

- the articles of incorporation of the company (a copy that is also with my law firm and my accountant)
- my hard copy file of current invoices

- my hard copy file of recent proposals
- my hard copy file of contract agreements
- my cheque books and related banking documents
- my list of credit card numbers and various access codes.
- credit cards, hotel and airline loyalty cards that I only use when travelling

---

Tip! It is also a great place to store your partner's jewellery collection when you go on holiday to a slightly 'iffy' part of the world.

- foreign currency (US dollars, Euros, Swiss francs etc.), which will pay taxi fares if necessary
- passports (the whole family), plus birth, marriage and other certificates
- contracts and claim forms for travel insurance, medical cover etc.
- CDs and floppy discs that back-up my computer, and copies of key manuscripts (books, research projects etc.).

Does it have a view?

This may sound silly to some – it's not. It is all about how you orientate your workspace. Why put yourself against a blank wall if you can position your worktop so that you can see out of a window (any window will do)? I believe that being able to see a patch of sky or the other side of the street lets you know there is a world out there. On some days, when things are not going too well, it helps – really!

My space – from hell to heaven

Five years ago, I was able to create my own workspace from the ground up – literally. Finding a house you love and being able to live in it is the real dream of many. We found that. The added bonus was an old artist's studio (like a small Victorian cricket pavilion) with huge, north-facing windows. Trouble was it was ready to fall down! After paying to have what I thought was going to be my new office taken down, I was left with a large 'footprint' to create a new workspace from the ground up.

One of the early lessons I learned was to think big. It doesn't really cost a great deal more (once you are signed up to build) to add extra space to the project. What I now occupy as working space is about the length and breadth of a static caravan – except this is an oak framed, timbered construction, roofed with reclaimed antique tiles. There is enough room inside for four or five desks if ever it were necessary, plus space for visitors. At the rear is a toilet and shower.

The concept I came up with was one that allows me to expand if required (without any additional capital outlay), but it also does two other things that need to be kept in mind.

It can be used in a completely different form. It could be transferred at little cost into a granny/guest apartment, games/billiard room etc. (all the facilities needed to do this are either installed or were plumbed/wired into the frame at construction). It has added hugely to the value of the whole property, making it especially interesting to anyone wanting to start or develop a business.

This IS important. Chances are you won't stay in your current location forever, so making your workspace not just attractive to you but desirable to others (no matter what they eventually use it for) is a great boost for the business.

While I appreciate only too well that not everyone has the room to do this to the extent I have been able to, keep your eyes very wide open. Instead of creating that 'super garden shed' style, is there another way? Could you get permission for two storeys? Could you dig down and create a basement and ground floor? Finally, don't be limited by what you see in catalogues. I had a local builder put my office together for approximately 50 per cent of the cost of those that advertise in the fancy catalogues and magazines. It pays to shop around.

... With One Enormous Chair

To paraphrase from the song 'Wouldn't it be Luverly' in the musical *My Fair Lady*, all I want is that enormous chair. You see, you can't sit at a desk staring at a VDU all day ... and possibly all night too. What you need are two things: stretch breaks (to postpone the day your body locks itself into a permanent stoop), and a big comfy chair (yes, that Ikea one will do fine) with a footstool. With that you can read papers, take breaks and generally be a little more civilised than the rest of toiling humanity may think you are. So when working on the workspace thing, try and get enough space for that too.

Also, don't forget that this is YOUR space, not THEIRS. Therefore you can do what you want. There is something really great about cranking up the music on a rainy February day (you just can't do that in an open plan office environment, can you?) and getting on with your work. Yes, when you get that first assignment, celebrate and go and buy a really good music centre.

Where do letterheads, pencils and printer ink come from?

If you have ever worked in an office environment, there's a good chance you don't know the answer to this question. Why? Because you never needed to know. You had heard rumours of a big cupboard somewhere, but that was all. Basically, it sort of arrived. Now you are on your own. So how do you go about buying all those accessories for your office?

Once again, the answer depends on what are you going to be doing:

- If you plan to use a lot of materials, run an account and get it delivered.
- If you are not at all sure, buy some and then work it out as you use it.

Tip! DANGER SIGNAL! People who have never been into an office supply super-store need to be accompanied by a responsible adult. You don't need all those paperclips, even if they are on offer – honest!

In my own case, I use a lot of paper and a lot of ink and frankly that's about it. So I bulk-buy these items and then once a year buy the rest on one trip to a big discount store. And despite being careful, I'll never use all those colourful paper-clips!

So, what do you need to stock a basic independent consultant's office with what used to be called stationery and supplies?

Printer paper ❏
Notepads ❏
Post-It Notes: several colours and sizes ❏
Envelopes: several sizes ❏
Envelopes: padded ❏
Envelopes for CD/diskettes ❏
Mailing tubes for large items ❏
Plastic folders ❏
Box files ❏
Stapler ❏
Staples ❏
Paper clips ❏
Bulldog clips ❏
Pens: several types and colours ❏
Pencils ❏
Eraser ❏
Marker pens ❏
Ruler, measuring tape ❏
Calculator for desk (large numbers) ❏
Calculator for pocket ❏
Scotch tape dispenser ❏
Scotch tape ❏
Adhesive tape for wrapping materials ❏

Rolodex and inserts (optional) ❏
Burnable CDs ❏
Blank diskettes ❏
'In and Out'-type trays ❏
Message/noticeboard and pins ❏
Paper adhesive ❏
Scissors ❏
Letter-opener ❏
Document punch ❏
Document binder machine (optional) and materials ❏
Letterheads ❏
Business cards ❏
Compliments slips ❏
Desk diary ❏
Wall planner (optional) ❏

Reference materials

Note: most of this is available on the Web in one form or another

Dictionary ❏
Thesaurus ❏
World atlas ❏
Local/national atlas/maps ❏
Transport timetables ❏

Back to THOSE Rules

Now we have an office and some workspace. What else do we need? RULES for a start! You will recall that I have already laid down the law on this in Chapter 1 (see pp. 16–17). However, I really don't think that this can be said enough – make sure you have rules for your workspace.

While you are not exactly in prison (although it can feel like that some days), you need to let those around you know when they have visiting rights. Basically my work area is mine unless I agree otherwise. And I keep it that way.

Despite that, things happen:

- Beware of clutter-creep. Things appear as your office becomes a storeroom for stuff that others don't know what to do with.
- Because you own all the Scotch-tape, scissors, etc., it is convenient to use your office as a 'wrapping room'.
- It becomes the convenient hidey-hole. Last Christmas all the presents ended up on my spare desk, plus those for the school Christmas party.
- Don't install a large fridge. I made the mistake of putting our upright fridge freezer in the back of the office. This creates opportunities for multiple visits.
- Learn to dread – and be politically deaf to – the phrase, 'Just put this in your office dear for a day or two.'

It's your office, your workspace, keep it that way! (Well, at least try.)

The challenge of staying connected

While we have discussed staying in touch in earlier chapters, what we haven't tackled yet is just what we need to do to keep ourselves in the front of our clients' minds. Today, the danger about writing on any of this is that there is a very real danger you will be out-of-date by tomorrow. My basic thought on this is that it really doesn't matter which method of staying in touch with your clients you go for, as long as:

- they can reach you when they need to
- everything you have is compatible with theirs.

We all know that technology is turning phones into computers, and vice versa. Our need to be in a fixed place to have a conversation or pass notes and images to each other has vanished. All the same, you are going to have to invest in one or two expensive basics to get you going.

So for most offices today we are talking about:

- a main computer (although you could use a laptop with a docking station)
- a laptop (or a combi with a mobile phone)
- a fixed-line phone (with two lines and broadband)
- a mobile phone
- a printer
- a scanner
- a fax.

There are multiple choices in the technology you need. What matters is how well it works for you. You can get into all sorts of discussions on this, but the easy way is to work backwards. Don't look at the hardware. Ask yourself, 'What do I need it for?' then find what fits best.

Let's use what I work with as an example.

I have a **main computer** (we have a total of three in a local area network). One is new, the others are just 'there' and get used from time to time. They are a useful legacy and still work fine – if slowly.

I have a **laptop** (a Sony Vaio), bought for the fact that it is fast, tough, very light, and has a long-battery life and a great keyboard (I create words as the number one activity, so that is a very important feature for me). As far as laptops go, I find the better the features the more you pay (weight and battery-life being premiums).

Tip! Every independent consultant needs two lines. You need to be able to answer while you are on the phone to another customer.

My **fixed-line phone** has two lines, plus my broadband (there is a fax line too, but linked onto the broadband line). I suppose that soon we won't need fixed lines and will be able to make do with mobiles. Right now I am waiting.

My **mobile phone** has good e-mail facilities. This means that on short trips (a day or two) I don't need to take my laptop. Equally, the mobile has to be able to go for two days without a recharge (although if you are smart, you'll know where to sneakily plug in your charger at restaurants and other public places). I have not embraced messaging as much as I possibly should, but then I'd still rather pick up a phone and talk than e-mail. Face it, consultants ARE supposed to talk to people. I just don't see that going out of style.

I have a **printer and scanner**, pretty basic, but they do the job. I have never been comfortable with those combination fax/printer/scanner machines. One part of the technology always seems to be woefully inadequate.

My **fax** I am convinced is obsolete, until the one time every month I need it. Recently, with e-mails getting lost a lot more (the way faxes used to), I have noticed a little more traffic. Today, faxes get attention, e-mails don't. So I'm not going to throw it away – yet.

Then, of course, I have **answering** and **call divert**, two lifelines, without which the independent consultant would just have to pay someone to do the job. Call divert is my main feature, allowing me to be 'in the office' wherever I am in the world. As I said earlier, for longer trips I use an answering service.

Staying ahead

The key to technology for me is to update it when you see either very real gain in doing so, or that you are in danger of falling behind the applications your clients use. The very real gain has to make something easier or faster, or you more accessible. Playing catch-up is just one of the investments you know you'll have to keep making. Personally, I think it is better to try and keep up incrementally than make big technical leaps. Somehow, those that do the latter never ever seem to catch up with the rest of us.

When you consider what the last two decades have brought in technology to the workplace, you have to be a little scared about what the next 20 will bring. Sitting here with my wireless keyboard and mouse, staring at my giant flat screen, with my broadband connection linking me to just about anything I want, it is easy to think I have the ultimate. But I know that more technologies are going to change that (I've already witnessed some at first-hand). I suppose the image revolution is next, allowing us to have live conversations on screen. This will really take off as soon as our clients seriously adopt it and we have to follow. How I am going to get around the fact that I am still at lunch (even if it is with another client) at four o'clock on a Friday I just don't know. Is this where technology ceases to be fun?

What, for me, is one of the biggest issues these days is the assumption made by others that technology works, when we know it is fallible. Too often these days, personal assistants send e-mails to cancel or re-arrange meetings when you are not in a position to pick up the message. Or it simply never gets to you.

Tip! I make a point of re-confirming every meeting or appointment 24 hours before the event. In today's disorganised world it is a good discipline to have.

But for the independent consultant being in touch is vital. Years ago we had assistants; today we tend to be on our own, because the technology has made it possible. But think, until someone comes up with time travel we can't be in two places at the same time. Technology will help us get, carry out and deliver the business, but it isn't the driver. It is only a very useful assistant to those of us who know how to use it properly and be unsurprised by its failings.

Get professional help

In all this, make certain you have access to professional help. No matter how good the gadgets and gizmos we have today are, a lot of them don't do quite what it says on the box. The professionals know (well they should!) what bits work best with what. They also know how to help in a crisis. So, as I have said before, make sure you have easy, face-to-face access with a knowledgeable IT expert. And remember, you will pay for what you get and YES, it can be too cheap!

The travelling consultant

Consultants were born to travel. Unless you are very lucky, as an independent you will be on the move for a large part of your professional time. That is how business gets secured, carried out and delivered. You may travel around your region, around the country, across Europe or all over the globe. Whatever happens, it is useful to set some standards, while always knowing that the client's own travel policies may occasionally prevail.

Getting prepared

Do you remember that song 'I Don't Like Mondays'? Well, I know – I think we all know – how Bob Geldof felt. Monday is never a great day, and down through history everyone from Churchill and Stalin (reputedly) to the cartoon cat Garfield has loathed it. If you are a traveller there is a good reason for that – it is NOT the day to go away. Why? Because everyone else wants to.

As I have got older (and maybe just a little wiser), I have begun to travel on Sunday. What this does is get me into a hotel at my Monday work location early to late evening. I get myself fully organised for the next day and I AM THERE. Too many times, I have faced the crush of an airport or rail station on a Monday only to be delayed. The end result is that you arrive at your client late and your entire schedule is ruined. This does not send good signals out to your client. So, even if it costs me (ie I pay the hotel night) I do it. That way I am always there, rested and effective.

Now there may well be good reasons for not doing that, but if you can, try it. It makes a lot of sense.

The other thing NOT to do is to come home on a Friday evening. Why? Because everyone else (or at least all those who haven't read this book) are on the road, in the train, on the plane. The worst place to be on a Friday night is a major airport or rail station. People just want to get home and don't mind how many toes they tread on doing it. If you can, come home on Thursday, or Friday morning.

As for preparation, I never (unless it is forced on me by circumstance) pack at the last minute. If I am leaving on a Sunday afternoon, I will get all my paperwork and technology (the laptop and attendant bits and pieces) ready at the end of the working day on Friday.

> Tip! I always travel with duplicate cables for Internet links, for the reason that I once got one stuck in a hotel room outlet and could not get it out without breaking it. Duplicate phone chargers make sense too. To make sure I never forget anything I have a plastic zip-lock bag with everything permanently packed inside. All I need to do is pick it up and put it in my carry-on case.

Travelling light

Let's face it: unless we are a movie star, it is inconvenient to take a lot of luggage. In fact, what we want to do (and the airlines in particular conspire continuously against us) is to be able to keep our bag with us at all times. Whether you can achieve that or not depends very much on your ability to pare down what you take with you. However, be careful. Except for day trips – and an occasional overnight where I know what I will be doing – I always take a spare pair of trousers (when someone has spilt melted butter on your only pair on the first evening of a two-day trip you learn!), and they have come in handy many times.

But these days – as I explained earlier – there are mini-protocols attached to what to wear (that's where those Oxford shirts work so well), so if you don't want to end up hauling a cabin trunk, here are some ideas.

Assuming that you are going to have business meetings, here's what I would pack for a two/three day trip.

- one suit (dark)
- three Oxford shirts (white or blue)
- one blazer or more casual jacket (travel in this) and trousers
- one casual shirt/lightweight roll-neck
- usual underclothing and socks
- real handkerchiefs
- one very lightweight bathrobe (do you really want to call housekeeping at eleven at night when you get to your room and find there isn't one?)

- light raincoat (spring, summer, autumn)
- heavy overcoat (winter).

What you need to achieve as a consultant is a sense of understated elegance and organisation. If I travel in a jacket and slacks I can always take just one pair of shoes, and the overcoat goes with both jacket and suit. I can add a tie to the shirt when I put on the suit and take it off in the evening.

I also have a miniature toilet bag (a tiny leather thing I got given by an airline about 20 years ago that seems to never wear out). I seek out anything in men's toiletries that are small (most manufacturers haven't a clue about this and could make a fortune if they tried a little harder). My toilet bag never gets emptied, just refilled, so it is always ready to drop into my travel gear at a moment's notice.

For shortish trips it usually contains:

- razor – smallest throwaway version available
- shaving cream – in a miniature canister
- aftershave – decanted into a small plastic bottle I discovered on my travels)
- deodorant – small version
- toothpaste – very small
- toothbrush – folds in two
- hairbrush (yes, still have some!) – also folds in two.

That's the basics for a two to three-day trip.

The two-suit trip

If you are going for longer then you do need more stuff, if only for variety. What I call a 'two-suit' trip is usually around 10 days. Other 'two-suit' trips for me are conferences, where you need to be seen in something different every day.

So you are going to need the big suitcase for this. But don't go crazy. Sure, pack the two suits, but then try and get by with a more casual jacket as travel/weekend wear. That light raincoat goes anywhere. Then take a second pair of shoes and possibly a pair of good light walking shoes. With that, you are fit for anything.

Shirts and stuff

Unless I am moving around a lot (that is, one night in one place and the next night in another), or in some totally inhospitable place, I never take more than around six shirts with me. You can save a lot of weight by getting them laundered at the hotel.

Keeping the weight down is definitely worthwhile, because it is one of those unexplainable laws of nature and business that you always end up bringing more paper and stuff back with you than you started with.

Luggage planning

This may sound really mundane, but get this wrong and you are headed for years of misery. Simply put, invest in some decent luggage for two reasons:

- It will last longer and probably have the features you need.
- Your client won't think that you are the only business he has and therefore try and cut your fees – again!

I have four pieces of luggage I can call on, depending on the circumstances of the trip:

- For day trips I have a computer bag (with double shoulder straps in case I am carrying a lot).
- For more formal day trips (and up to three-day trips), I have a leather bag that has expanding sides as well as a matching small laptop bag that fits inside. The way it is laid out means I can get all my papers in one part and all my personal items in the other (many of my independent peers find what are known as airline pilot's cases a useful equivalent). It has a padded shoulder strap and works well and looks better and better the older it gets.
- I have an (on-wheels) suit-bag. This is like those little wheelie-cases that should go in overhead lockers but never do. Except this does keep suits and jackets in a well-pressed condition, and has an expansion area so I can put my overcoat in there too if I need it. I have also reached the stage where I check in items and keep the critical stuff (including my miniaturised toilet bag) with me in my leather bag. That way, if my bag gets lost (which in truth has only happened once in the last five years) I have a fresh shirt etc., so I can go see clients without any problems. And yes, I always carry my laptop with me.
- I have a monster, all-wheel Samsonite. This is the 'off-road', 4x4, mother of all suitcases and comes out only for the big events where lots of clothes and work materials are needed.

Travelling with clients

Over the years, I must have read a zillion words about management and doing business. Never in all that time have I read anything about one of the toughest assignments you can ever get – travelling with your client. I mean, so conscious are we about ourselves that even the venerated journal the *Harvard Business Review* has begun featuring in-depth 'Managing Yourself' articles. But nowhere is there any mention of one of life's most challenging moments: sharing a train, plane or automobile with your client (they don't even mention it for the boss–subordinate relationship). But believe me, this is really hard work.

To give you an idea of what is involved, it is similar to going on holiday for the first (and only) time with your best friend. They just aren't the same person one they have stepped on that plane. The same applies entirely to your client.

In the course of my professional career as an independent consultant, I have been to conferences, tradeshows and roadshows with clients. And I have watched in a state akin to horror as these people change like monsters in one of those cheap horror movies.

For some it is party, party, party. For others it is girls, girls, girls. Others still, gamble, gamble, gamble. I have lost count of all the mild-mannered Clark Kents I have chaperoned over the years – except they don't turn into Superman, but one of his evil enemies instead. Then you get back and the first day you visit after the horrors of the tradeshow or whatever, it is like nothing ever happened. My advice is *nothing ever happened*!

My other advice is that most often they want you to lead them along, and find the taxis and the places you are due to visit. So even if they are nursing the world's greatest hangover, you don't want to be. My trick, honed to a fine art over thousands of unwanted late-night sessions, is to VANISH. I will appear to be headed for the toilets and I just don't come back. I go to bed and stay there. When it gets to bale-out time, everyone else is too preoccupied or, frankly, beyond rational thought, to remember when you packed it in. If there is anyone rankled that you are fighting fit and ready to go the following day, they will soon appreciate your ability to get things organised.

Having said that, I have had many great times on tour with clients. But they are not always people whom you would naturally make friends with in private life. Professional commitments throw all sorts of people together. What you need to do is make certain you can get some down-time and escape to your hotel room to decompress. Believe me, it is necessary.

Travel rules for independents

Whether you are travelling around your own country or across the world for your job, some basic rules apply. Most of these we pick up by bitter experience as we develop our businesses. Others are simple, common sense.

My number one rule is that I always travel the day before a critical meeting. And as I have said earlier, Sunday evenings are far more civilised times to travel than the mania of a Monday morning. In my early days working on my own, I recall the regular horror of realising that there was a delay caused by 'something' that meant I wouldn't make that critical meeting (and, therefore, none of the others I had built around it either).

Yes, it will cost a little more, but I have found that clients appreciate people who show up on time. Also, when you have time in your hotel room you can get a lot of things done. Or, as a lot of my friends do, just unwind for a few hours. As many of these people, who have busy professional and private lives, say, 'You have no idea how much I appreciate a few hours on my own.'

> ### What time, which city?
>
> This is a very important tip for anyone who has an international portfolio to juggle. Make sure that anyone who helps you realises that the world is broken down into time zones! Seem logical – but no, it's not. Assistants get it wrong all the time. If you have any doubts there is a great website – www.timeanddate.com. This allows you to input the name of your location and it works out actual times against other global locations. This is terrific if you have to have a conference call between Memphis, Manchester and Mumbai, as it will show you the optimum times to do it.

Getting the best deals

Independent professionals are some of the most sinned-against travellers. In fact, we probably keep the airlines and hotel chains in business. Big corporate clients get travel deals that we poor solo workers can only dream of. So it means that we need to carefully consider how we book our travel.

If you have a good relationship with your clients, you can always ask them to book you into hotels at their rate. This can save you anything from 25 to 50 per cent on what you might pay.

The same goes for air travel. Many of my own clients have automatic upgrades from full-fare economy to business for long-haul travel. So it does pay to ask.

The other thing to do is find hotels that you like and do deals with them. Usually if you can commit to between 15 and 20 days each year, they'll be happy to discount your room (often to a significant degree). My belief has always been in finding a good hotel in an area you like and then asking for a meeting with the manager. If the hotel is any good, they'll know who you are and be happy to do a deal.

Certainly, if you are going to be in a city for a good number of days a year you want a place to stay that gives you some home comforts and some feeling of a 'home-away-from-home' each time you arrive.

In choosing hotels (unless my client is kind enough to help me out), I look for a series of things:

- easy transport access
- good lobby, informal areas for meetings
- room with a working desk
- a quiet room location at the back (I don't care about the view if there's a major street outside!)
- room service
- fast laundry facility
- low turnover of staff (so they know you and you know them)
- a 'neighbourhood' location, where you can find small restaurants and bars (and breakfast) to avoid exorbitant hotel dining 'experiences.'[8]

Now this may add a little to your travel budget, but it is worth it. Cheap hotels are rarely that cheap. If you shun the five-star 'palaces' and check out carefully three- and four-star places, you'll soon find a place that you like, and that is very liveable. Often, after I have 'discovered' these places my clients use them too!

However, remember that it has to be a place where you can meet your clients and prospects without you looking like a down-at-heel shoe salesman. So choice is vital, it says a lot about you.

And don't forget that a host of Internet sites offer great deals too. I have become a serial user of sites like www.laterooms.com and www.expedia.com, just because they offer such great deals for the independent consultant. I was delighted recently when I met an old friend in the lobby of a seriously expensive five-star hotel to discover that my late room deal was 50 per cent cheaper than his organisation's corporate rate!

To book or not to book

It is strange to think that a few years ago I wouldn't be (couldn't be) writing this section at all. Yet such has been the enormous take-up of the Internet

---

[8] In any major city in Europe a good quality hotel charges £15 (€20) and upwards for breakfast. In London, Paris, Brussels, Amsterdam and Zurich I have friendly cafes two minutes walk from my regular hotels where I can eat better for less than £5 (€7.50). And they are a lot more fun.

that most independents I know have eschewed their travel agents and moved on to do it themselves.

Certainly, after decades of dealing with a travel agent (and spending upwards of £15,000 a year with them), I haven't used one in the last year. Why?

- They charge around £20 (€30) per ticket they issue.
- I can – and have – found cheaper deals than the ones they offer
- The only time this isn't true (and this is already changing as I write) is for multiple destination trips and interlining (using more than one airline). Of course it does take time to do the research, but as most consultants I know tend to go back to specific places (at least for the period of a contract or assignment), once the basics are plugged into your 'favourites' it takes seconds to make a reservation the second and subsequent times.

Welcome to the throw-away society

With on-line booking so prevalent, I have also discovered that it is better to 'buy' non-refundable tickets and take the chance on something changing rather than pay the premium for fully-flexible tickets. For most airlines and other travel operators, the difference is usually around 50 per cent. For those of us

> *Tip! Just as with hotels, cheap options on local travel can turn out expensive. If I am spending a lot of time in one place I usually locate a car and driver, because at the end of the day, they cost very little more than a dirty taxi. It also means you don't queue at airports and you can plan your out-of-town client visits meticulously.*

who travel considerably, having to throw away the odd reservation still makes our travel much, much cheaper than a few years ago. This means that any independent consultant can afford to prospect a lot more broadly than before.

Charging travel time

I know of very few independent consultants who charge travel time 'up front'; usually it gets built into proposals one way or another. However, if a client sends you off around a series of towns or cities, then they should be paying for the block of time they are taking up. The same

> *Tip! Unless I have no option but to get into a location and out again at speed, I will always try and see at least one other 'contact' whenever I travel. First, it keeps up – or adds to – your network. Second, you just might get lucky. Strangely enough, I have often picked up business for the sole reason that I was the person in a prospect's office when an assignment cropped up.*

applies to expenses. I charge travel expenses when I am travelling for a client, but not to go and see them if I am in a different location from them. As I indicated earlier in discussing development costs, the smart independent consultant needs to know how to 'massage' these kinds of costs into the overall assignment. Sadly, some will for ever remain 'sunk' costs. This is the price of doing business today.

Expenses on the road

I would imagine that everyone has their own rules for keeping track of expenses on the road. Mine are very simple. I only ever use American Express for business travel (with a MasterCard back-up for those annoying places where they refuse Amex!). Any cash transactions are paid for with my own money, and expensed to the business on my return.

In an age that boasts instant access to credit cards, my choice of Amex as a business card is simple:

- They are very efficient.
- They have a great reward programme (and the points don't expire).
- They have a card that gets you free access into airline lounges (priceless!).
- If you clear your charges every month you have unlimited credit (necessary for travel).

(When I moved from Belgium to the UK, my MasterCard-issuing bank (who refused to call my bank in Brussels, where I had banked for 20 years) offered me a maximum of £2,500 credit on my card. You can probably see why I didn't use them.)

As with everything else in an independent's existence, you have to seek out the things that work for you in your situation. But by keeping business costs and personal costs separate, you won't spend hours trying to work out what is what.

That, for example, is why I usually insist on buying my own tickets – unless a client has a steal of a deal. First it means that you are always flexible and can change your travel plans up to the very last minute (something many independents have to do); second, you can rack up those points.

Staying in touch on the road

I have talked about this earlier, but can never stress enough that being 'available' is one of the critical aspects of the independent consultant's life. You can possibly get away with being relaxed about other aspects of the business, but being reachable is set in stone. It is the very foundation of our existence.

Beware the geographically challenged

If you do use external help or get busy enough to hire a part-time or full-time assistant, make sure that they understand that there is a big world out there that has different times and stuff.

Two things that happened to me illustrate this:

I was in Tokyo and had just fallen asleep when there was a whirring noise close to my ear. I was convinced there was some fairly lethal insect about to attack. Flinging off the covers, I grabbed a shoe and dashed around the room – only to discover, neatly tucked away in a cupboard, a fax machine, on which my new assistant back in Europe was sending me a message. For me it was almost midnight, for her it was four in the afternoon!

I had recruited a young, enthusiastic graduate who had excelled in everything I gave him to do. Part as reward and part as further training, I sent him off to meet with one of my clients in the USA. We flew together to London, where he was to board his transatlantic flight. As a novice global trekker, he asked me to look at his ticket to work out which terminal in Heathrow he was to leave from. Lucky he did. He was supposed to be going to Portland, Maine, via Boston. He had a ticket for Portland, Oregon, via Seattle! Our new assistant had done it again!

Getting a reputation for being difficult or (God forbid) impossible to reach is a death knell. So, yes, mobile phones are a lifeline, especially if they are compatible with your laptop.

Having said that, don't think I am suggesting that you never switch off – on the contrary. But just make sure that you have surrounded yourself with the people and technology that make it possible for you to respond to five alarm fires from your palm bedecked beach in the Caribbean.

As I pointed out earlier in the book, call diverts, message services, and mail diverts are all available – there's just no excuse these days to be 'missing and out of the action.'

The workplace IS everywhere 1: the airline lounge

Virtually all the solo consultants I know are as at home in an airline lounge as anywhere else. Incidentally, it is worthwhile having access to lounges (the service that American Express accords me is excellent because it isn't down to which airline you are flying). Most access gets restricted to which level of traveller each individual airline considers you to be. This means that if you suddenly find yourself on 10 return trips to Edinburgh, you never build up enough equity in the so-called frequent flyer programme to use anything. Then, just as your client's assignment is over, the airline sends you a card that gives you lounge access in an airport you will probably never go to again!

I have hung out in airport lounges in snowstorms and strikes. And although they can get a bit crowded at peak travel times, they can offer a quiet place to sit and work. Also, I have made it my business to find a little oasis of calm in all the airports I regularly use. There are always some, even on the busiest day in the summer, where you can squirrel yourself away and ignore the rest of seething humanity.

Tip! All the good 'corners' I know also have wall sockets, which mean you can charge your laptop and mobile phone – especially handy if you are delayed for a while.

The workplace IS everywhere 2: the hotel lobby

One highly successful independent management consultant I know does NOT have an office: never has, never will. His entire working life – in which he meets hundreds of people – takes place in the lobbies of Europe's most business-friendly hotels. Please note the 'business-friendly' tag, for this is important.

What you need are hotel lobbies where you can have a discreet discussion, and order breakfast, coffees, light lunches, tea and the odd glass of wine, without any eyebrows being raised. Sure, these 'friendly' locations occasionally disappoint (usually new management), but there are some that have given him, and myself, hundreds of hours of good service.

In some cases it might be a place you stay, but most of the time, it is a location that the person you are meeting can easily find and be impressed by your choice of venue. When you consider that most of us meet one-on-one or in fairly small groups, renting meeting rooms is a chore and costs money. The whole idea is to keep costs down (that other motto of the successful independent operator).

Clubs and professional associations can offer similar facilities, but so many of them frown on the active process of a business discussion that they usually ban any papers or other indications of commercial activity taking place.

Tip! Make sure you stake your claim to a prime space early: after the morning tourist rush is best.

Most important for this sort of thing to be successful is to look like you belong. Confidence is of the essence. And as long as you buy the occasional breakfast and the odd glass of wine for your 'guests', the smart hotelier will leave you to get on with your business.

Don't forget that the hotel is also a source of other 'services'. You can have courier deliveries sent there (well, you could be checking in) if you are travelling, and you can order taxis (especially useful when it is raining).

The workplace IS everywhere 3: public places

Increasingly we live in a comfort-obsessed society, and so more and more 'spaces' are open for the use of us travelling people. Recently, I have been compiling a list of art galleries, museums and other public spaces that have seating areas and food and drink available too (many also have free Internet connections and wireless LAN). Begin to compile your own list of places. You will be surprised by just how many are perfect for interviews and discussions with clients.

The workplace IS everywhere 4: restaurants

'Doing lunch' is a major part of the independent consultant's mating dance. Again, what you want is a place that impresses your contact (without depressing your bank account) and makes him or her feel at ease. What I have done is to patronise a regular set of places where I am known well enough to get that slightly better table. There are two sure-fire ways to do this:

- Get there early (and use the time to pre-brief yourself) and just ask for a bigger, or more discreet table.
- Be really naughty and book a table for three (means you'll get a table for four) when there are only two of you.

What I look for in a restaurant is a place with well-spaced tables, so your conversation doesn't spill into the next group (bistros are not good places to meet). My favourites are eating places with booths, where you can settle in for a long session and ignore the rest of the world.

The workplace IS everywhere 5: OPOs (other people's offices)

Why so few people think of this I don't know. OPOs are THE very best really, but only work if you have put that hard work into developing your network. I have a host of non-competing independent consultants who are only too delighted to let me borrow an office, even for a meeting with one of my clients. As long as the offices don't look like they are about to be condemned by a building surveyor, they actually can help a client relationship. The client realises that you 'know' people and this is usually deemed to be a 'good thing'. Similarly, your kind friend who has loaned you a meeting room or whatever hopefully thinks that this may be an opportunity for them too. My, my, free office coffee never tasted so good!

The workplace IS everywhere 6: the final solution!

Finally one that most people may never consider, but is truly fantastic, offering privacy, security and a spotless environment in which to work – the rest rooms of very good hotels! Over the years, I have carefully kept a note of the best loos in most cities in Europe (and quite a few in the USA too). These are rest rooms that are not fully manned, so they don't see you go in. But they are the ones that get cleaned every 30 or 60 minutes (there's always a checklist on the back of the entrance door to prove it). Large stalls, fully air-conditioned, a hook to hang your coat, and good locations also have a window-ledge or other place to put your bag. Good ones also (even in basements) have mobile phone access. I know this may seem a bizarre choice, but it works well (remember, they have to be spotless!).

An ongoing challenge

With more and more people taking the plunge into independent life, finding quiet corners to work will take increasing ingenuity. The other day, I was in a business club in London, and it was full at 10 o'clock– quite horrible. A two-minute walk away was a delightful (practically deserted) public library with a coffee shop attached and comfortable chairs! Where would you rather be? Chances are that for many of us, life as an independent is going to mean a lot of time on the road. In doing this we can make it pleasant or just plain purgatory. Take a little time to discover what's really available around where you need to meet people. You'll be surprised what you'll find (and, I imagine, delighted too).

Key learning points

- Can you work from home, or close by? If you can great, it keeps down costs and commuting time.
- You MUST have a dedicated area in your home that is safe, secure and where you can work undisturbed.
- Try and have an external access to your office. It is better for deliveries, visiting clients and creating a climate of professionalism.
- If you are going to build a workspace in your garden check it out with the neighbours and make sure you don't need official permission.

- Put in a toilet facility and running water and be able to heat AND cool the property.
- Make sure you have room to expand, as the business grows or for storage space.
- If home alone isn't for you, are there nearby office facilities that you can rent or share with other professionals?
- Don't regret it later: buy a safe and make sure it is fireproof and heavy.
- Get comfy! Apart from a good desk chair you need a nice big upholstered chair to do your thinking in.
- Be careful with office supplies. You can buy too much – easily!
- You are the office, you have to stay connected wherever you are.
- Just because you are on your own doesn't mean you can stop learning – keep as up-to-date as you can, and that goes for your equipment too.
- Learn to travel light and to travel smart. Try to leave on days that are less busy.
- Negotiate hotel deals if you go back to locations on a regular basis, or get your clients' corporate rate.
- Better to buy cheap tickets and occasionally throw them away than buy fully flexible at a huge premium.
- For 'on the road' expenses, develop a system to keep track of your costs and stick to it.
- Remember, today the workplace is everywhere: learn to recognise and use those 'free' corners of airports, hotels and the rest.

Chapter 4

Life of a salesman

Whenever you're sitting across from some important person, always picture them sitting in their underwear. That's the way I always operated in business.

Joe Kennedy

The customer's always right,
The son of a bitch
Is probably rich
So smile with all your might.

Noel Coward

Selling yourself

To a great extent, this chapter is probably the most important of all. Why? Well, if you can't sell yourself, your product or your service, no great idea, genius level IQ, hard work, smart offices or really well-organised administrative system are going to do you any good at all. Being perfectly honest, if you can't sell you don't eat.

In more than two decades of selling myself most days in one way or another, I have seen so many highly successful people fail on the very basic issue of being able to sell effectively. To my mind there are four pillars of failure. If you recognise yourself in one of these, please think long and hard about your next step.

Selling failure 1: you think selling is sleazy

The attitude that selling puts you at the level of a really pushy used car salesman is far more common than you would think. Many good professionals don't realise when they begin the going-it-alone process that the sell is really the key part, and a lot of them find it beneath their dignity. Strangely, selling does not come naturally to many of us. There are very few born salesmen, and if they are good they should stick to that and that alone. But for professional executives, having to beat a path to a prospect is not a natural thing to do. Many make the huge mistake of thinking that customers will somehow track them down. Honest – it won't happen. You need to realise that all the comfort factors of a regular job are not there anymore. And just as you will have to learn to queue up at the post office to buy your stamps, so you will have to realise that the sell is the key to survival. So while it may be unnatural, without it you don't succeed.

Selling failure 2: you forget to sell

Are you shaking your head? Asking, 'What does he mean by that?' Well, every week I see people who get busy and forget to sell (mainly because deep down they don't want to anyway). And it is so easy to fall into this trap. 'Wow, I'm really busy, got to keep at it.' Then, one day, you have shipped your last product, written your last report, sent your last invoice – and it is another kind of 'Wow' altogether. It is the 'Wowwwwwwwwwww' that comes from the echo of the empty store cupboard. Over the years I have seen so many newly minted independents fail because they got busy initially and forgot to prime the pump. No pipeline, no work. And believe me, it is harder to generate work when you have to. So remember what I explained in Chapter 2: no matter how busy you get, devote a set amount of time to business development – and that includes selling.

Selling failure 3: you can't ask for the order

This, of course is the classic. So many of us have a deep-seated psychological hang-up about actually asking for the order. We are not the type of people who have Bob Geldof moments and shout, 'Give us the fucking money!' Most of us – if truth were known – are timid creatures at heart, and we are scared to ask. While a little later in this chapter I'll talk about the psychology of when to ask, you need to realise right from the start that being unable to ask for the order is going to disqualify you from joining the ranks of the sole trader. All the time, I see bright, energetic independents coming a real cropper through their inability to say, 'So have you reached a decision yet, can we get started?' The main reason for this works as follows. You have put a proposal into the XYZ Group. You've discussed it, modified it, trimmed your fees. You've done everything and you still haven't got a go-ahead. BUT, as long as you don't ask, they haven't said no. So you wait, for the simple reason that you don't want to hear bad news.

Often, you will find that there are reasons for the delay. But the most important point is that if you haven't the confidence and the basic chutzpah to push for a decision, this will tell your prospective client that you are not at all sure of yourself. So screw up your courage and make the call. Either way, you will know and you can then get on with your life.

Selling failure 4: chemistry

Every book about selling says the same thing. When you meet a prospect, the first 30 seconds determine your ultimate fate. And it is usually very simple. If they like you it's OK. If they don't, you may as well go home now (prospects are rarely, if ever, indifferent). So the key here is to get to know the signs and get out if you have to. No matter how juicy that project may be, if you are honest with yourself, you'll never get it, not in a million years. Then again, over my career there are probably hundreds of times when I have got on so well with a prospect that I have been given more work than I went for (often, much of it I was not even qualified to do!). However, if you know that you don't come across well in front of prospects or don't really like meeting new people, maybe this line of work isn't for you.

On the other hand, if you think that you can sell, and have a winning way with prospects, let's move on and see what we are going to call your fledgling venture. Or, perhaps more importantly, what do you want the market to think you are?

Oh no! Not another logo!

Over the years I have collected literally thousands of business cards from one-man outfits trying to appear the size of General Motors. Let me give you this tip from the outset: it's a waste of time. Why? Because what people are buying is YOU. Your reputation, your skill.

I once knew a manager who had been terminated (I think I know why) and who spent the first week of his new career as an independent creating a name for the company, designing a logo and then getting the whole caboodle of letterheads, envelopes, business cards, order forms, brochures and the like printed. Then he realised he wasn't any good at it and got another job.

Here's my advice for naming your company: what's your name? Use that.

No, I don't mean use it as it is, but make it sound important. Like this:

- Johnson & Associates
- The Johnson Group
- Johnson & Partners
- Johnson Consulting

Then attach – for the letterhead at least – a qualifying line about what you do:

- Consultants and Engineers
- Accountants and Tax Advisers
- Consultants in Corporate Social Responsibility
- Defining Marketing Strategy
- Changing Corporate Communications

Don't make the second line about what you do too limiting – you never know which way business opportunity will lead you. You need a flexible, slightly ambiguous title that looks important. Never, ever tie yourself down. As anyone who has been in business for themselves for some years has discovered, you will find your business evolves (not necessarily in the way you plan it, either!).

This uncontrolled metamorphosis of a business happens for two reasons. First, you gain more expertise as you develop, and this will lead you to new opportunities. Second, trends are just that: what you have started out doing may have a very definite shelf-life, and you need to be able to adapt your offering to suit the changing market. If you lock yourself down with a too tightly defined name, you'll strangle opportunity.

Of course, you can call yourself the Acme Consulting Group (chances are there is one already), but over the years I have found using your own name and a suitable qualifying descriptor works best, at least in the initial stages.

Having said that, neither do you want to make your operation look too small. So giving yourself a title on the card like Managing Partner, Senior Consultant and the like helps too. Additionally, being seen as part of some national or international network gives the whole show a sense of solemn purpose. While it may sound silly or self-evident, I know of hundreds of sole traders who have 'relationships' with other consultants and seem to feel that this is all you require to have a letterhead with half of the capital cities of the world on the bottom! But there is some real method to this sort of madness. Many large companies don't like working with sole traders (some even have policies relating to this), and simply feel they need to know there is some kind of back-up available if things go wrong.

> *Tip! Don't forget that registering names is critical. Get your accountant to do it for you. This means that they will do a full search to see if the name is available for use. Also make sure that your URL is fully registered. Depending what you are going to be doing in a professional capacity, it is probably worth registering www.XYZ.com, www.XYZ.co.uk (or whatever country you are using) as well as www.XYZ.org. These will cover you for the future and make sure that no one else can use them.*

My first lesson in this sort of corporate subterfuge came back in 1982, my first year as an independent. I was asked to do some fairly intensive and confidential work for a major oil company. A consulting firm in New York with whom I was partnered made it clear that my chances of getting any more business were minimal unless I changed my letterhead. That day, out went my beautiful letterhead with an italic script 'Mike Johnson' followed by 'Writer and Consultant'; in came 'Johnson & Associates Limited: Consultants in Corporate Communication'. On the letterhead was my name, 'Michael A. Johnson', with the grand title 'Managing Partner' underneath.

Certainly I was still the same, but I had learned something important. If you want to appeal to corporations (large or small), you've got to make them feel comfortable. It is a lesson I have never forgotten. Play their game, not yours. They want to believe you are part of them, so do it. It doesn't hurt at all, just makes you all the more professional (and most probably more expensive to hire).

Sorry, I've got the decorators in – again!

My very first 'office' was the spare bedroom of my apartment in Brussels. While carrying out a series of assignments for a large US multinational, there was a visiting senior vice-president who kept wanting to come over and meet in my office. For six months the decorators were in residence, possibly the longest painting job in history! I got the message and quickly leased a second apartment in the same building to use as offices. It meant commuting a few floors to work each day, but at last I was able to present a well kitted-out corporate front.

All this is about learning 'the Game'. The Game is never played the way it seems to be when you are employed. But the Game is your day-to-day reality.

Tip! If you can work close, but not 'at' home, do it. You'll save time, commuting costs and much frustration.

What you have to be able to do is make your clients and prospects consider you to be one of them.

Do I dress for success?

So, you're an independent consultant. How do you dress? Are there any rules these days that need to be followed? As far as I am concerned, there is only one.

Dress to show that you respect your client and his or her environment.

If you want a second rule, this is my own:

When in doubt, overdress – you can always take something off!

Let me explain this a little.

Twenty years ago, life was pretty easy in the sartorial stakes. You wore a suit and tie and that was that. If you were in a serious profession, that suit was probably dark; if you were in a more liberal profession, you might have run to light grey. Today things are different.

My clients vary by industry, geography and size. They all have their dress codes and sub-dress codes. However, my rule is number one above: dress to show that you respect your client and his or her environment. By this I mean that if I am going into a good, solid professional firm where everyone wears suits and ties, I will too. If I am going into a new media environment where everyone wears jeans and t-shirts, I won't wear that (at my age I'd look ridiculous!), but I won't wear the tie.

On that basis I have refined my wardrobe along a sort of 'fitting in with the scenery' approach. And as I frequently travel and meet different groups with different dress rules and expectations, it has ended up as something like this:

- a dark suit that I wear with white or blue button-down Oxford shirts
- an innocuous blue blazer, that I can wear with or without a tie, and with one of the Oxford shirts mentioned above and a pair of either khaki or (if slightly more formal) grey trousers
- a grey herringbone cashmere jacket that travels well, worn with black or blue trousers (even from the suit above)
- a couple of dark, polo shirts that fit with the blazer if necessary
- (in summer) a long, beige trench-coat
- (in winter) a heavier grey or black suit with black roll-necks of very fine cotton (when not sticking to the Oxford shirts) and a heavy black overcoat.

Using this easy-to-travel mix, you can get just about anywhere.

For women, I often think it is even easier. One dark suit and lots of those white T-shirt style tops. Two pairs of shoes, including one sensible pair for walking the miles of corporate corridors and airport walkways. Coats, much of the same.

You may not come across like a Dior model, but you will be very efficient and look just the way you need to for whichever client crops up.

Whose rules?

To be considered 'one of them' you have to learn their rules. Trouble is, if you have five or six clients, you need to learn and follow five or six sets of rules – not slavishly, but certainly enough to gain their respect. I wish I could begin to tell you how many bloody corporate acronyms I have learned in 20-plus years. Why do every company and every industry have to have their own little codes for everything? I know that Bill Gates is rich and that lots of people seem to dislike him for it. But he has given us a basic standard for most of the systems we use. Early on, it was a nightmare trying to get anything to interface.

So, the rules are those that your clients play by. These are their touchstones, the things that make them feel good. If you want to play in their sandbox, learn the sandbox rules.

Confidence is a keyword

Exuding confidence, even when things are going rapidly awry, is a key attribute of the successful independent consultant. Strangely enough, many clients will look to you when they are unsure of themselves. As an external adviser, you are often there to shore up their own lack of ability, vision or whatever. Never, ever look confused, lost or out of your depth. As an old friend of mine once said, 'If you look poor, needy or desperate, you'll smell like a staked goat to a tiger.' Not a particularly nice allusion but right on the money! Clients can smell fear a mile away. And they don't like it any more than you do. They want to work with people who are confident, full of energy and ideas. Again, if you've got the mother of all hangovers, call in sick. It is the best – and hopefully only – decision you'll make that day. Better to lose one or two days' fees than the whole business – really.

Learn to ask for the business

As I pointed out earlier in this chapter, you've got to learn to 'ask' for the business as a standard part of your routine. And that act of asking is driven by confidence in your abilities. 'Of course they should give me the business, I'm good at this stuff' is the attitude to take. If you avoid asking, they'll just think that you don't believe enough in yourself or your service to demand the business. They'll think you are not really worth the fee or, perhaps, not ready for this level of responsibility.

Key learning points

- If you can't sell then you don't belong in the independent consulting game.
- You need to know how to 'ask for the order'.
- When deciding what to call your new business, keep it simple and flexible: think of the future and don't box yourself in.
- Registering your chosen name is critical.
- Try to appear substantial. Big corporations like to work with people who appear to have back-up.
- Be careful how you dress: keep it simple and smart.
- Learn to learn the clients' rules and play by them.

Chapter 5

Marketing yourself

Well, hopefully by now you are on your way. You've made a proposal, boldly asked for the order and been rewarded with some work. What you have done is to effectively 'sell' yourself. Now we need to move on and think about marketing yourself. For the independent consultant, this means putting yourself into a position where you get noticed – even sought out – by prospective clients. Is this really marketing? Well, yes and no. Frankly I think it is more personal public relations. You are creating a soft-sell ambience for yourself. Remember: the product is YOU.

To illustrate: I have a note on my wall that is by now dog-eared and faded with age, but which is a little piece of advice that I have found worthwhile to refer to from time-to-time. This is what it says:

If a boy meets a girl and he tells her how beautiful she is, how much he loves her and how he can't live without her – that's sales promotion.

If a boy meets a girl and immediately impresses upon her how wonderful he is – that's advertising.

But, if the girl seeks him out because she has heard from others what a fine chap he really is – that's public relations.

And that is what I think we independent consultants should aspire to in our self-marketing and business development. Our reputation is our best weapon for gaining business. The trick is how to enhance it.

Some people are born business developers. They just seem to make it very easy indeed. But on observing those types, I find that this apparent effortlessness is based on a lot of hard work. I have a work colleague who would get business if he crashed in the middle of the Amazon jungle or the Gobi desert. Most of us don't have that inbred talent. So unless you are a business generating dynamo, here are some thoughts and experiences that may help you get to the next step. These are not in any order of importance. Nor do I suggest you try and do them all. Just pick some of those that look like they'll work for you in your personal situation.

Sales materials – how much, how soon?

Luckily for anyone entering the world of the independent consultant today, the technology revolution has made a lot of what us oldies needed obsolete. More than that, the quality of office scanners, printers and copiers means that we can produce a great deal for ourselves (if we have the time and talent to do it).

Quite frankly, how much you create and how you create it depends solely on the business you are in. My own view is that unless you really have a need to impress, or do mass sales campaigns, keep your money in your pocket and forget the glossy brochure – no one reads it.

Add to that what I said a lot earlier; don't waste hours trying to create a desktop brochure or presentation pack if you haven't got the skills to do it. Get an expert and pay them – it will save you money in the long run.

In my view (although as I said this might not apply to your business), to get started you need the following:

- a business card (the best quality you can afford)
- a letterhead on best-quality paper. My advice is to get your company name printed in colour on the paper, but print out all the details – address, phone, bank, VAT etc. – from your computer. Why? They will change and this will keep you flexible and save money.
- envelopes, in various sizes and weights. Again, use your computer to print the address etc. Only geeks examine envelopes!
- an ink stamp with the name and address on, for bulky packages
- a compliments slip that can double up as a notelet, or be clipped to documents
- the best website your money can buy (see next page).

Print your way to oblivion

Here's a lesson. I had a friend who was made redundant from his high-powered job as a very senior human resource professional. He was generously compensated. His dream had always been to work as an independent in creating new learning environments for employees. Using his redundancy pay-out he set up the company, which initially had some small success. Encouraged, he began to produce marketing and sales material of incredible quality. It was so good that when I first saw it I thought it was from a big consulting firm. A book (which he paid to be published) followed, plus position papers and reports – all with the same high production (and high cost) values. Then one day, there was no money coming in, and the materials he had so carefully crafted (when he should have been out selling) were getting out-of-date. He is now back in the corporate world again. What he failed to see was that he created too much of a good thing. His material was too glossy, and creating it took too much time from what should have been the main focus.

The website

For virtually all independents, your website is THE marketing tool. Unless your granny left you a million pounds, forget brochures and other print. Spend your money on a website that does you proud. I make no apologies, I am going to keep hammering on this no brochure thing. You don't need them until you are rich, and then they are just an ego trip masquerading as a ludicrous indulgence.

To my mind, the website is the electronic version of the corporate brochure anyway. The beauty of it is that is doesn't cost thousands to change and fix.

Here are my tips on setting up your website:

- Preferably find someone you can easily go round and see face-to-face. Check them out with others and see just how good they are.
- Make sure YOU, not them, have all the access codes, or at least a way to get at them easily.
- Register your URL in as many ways as you can: the Web isn't going away, and the more bits you own the more flexible you can be.
- Make sure your designer isn't some charlatan with a Mac and little else in the technique department. We are in business here, not trying to imitate Andy Warhol.
- Visit frequently and then plan your update material so as to keep down costs. I do it once a month.
- Keep it simple, simple, simple. Especially on the home page, less is more.

The electronic calling-card par excellence

For me, a website is your showroom. In fact, it is a lot more than that: it not only shows what you can do – it vouches for you. Time after time I am on the phone trying to agree meetings, set up interviews and so on and the person I am calling will say, 'Yes, I'm on your website, I see who you are now.' This is a kind of security system. It is no good blagging your way in anymore. All people do is say, 'What's your site?' And you can't say, 'Well, I don't have one' – everyone has one (my neighbour's dog has one, for goodness' sake!).

Tip! What your website does is give you instant credibility, something that could take years to establish before this great invention. It is therefore possibly the greatest aid to the independent consultant ever devised.

Learn to link

There are ever more opportunities to extend your credibility through linking your website to other sites that underscore your excellence as a consultant.

Publish an article and it not only goes on your website, it is on the publisher's site too. Agree to speak at a conference, and it is on the event's pre- and post-report sites as well.

This leads me into one area that is very important. All of us hate making cold calls. But if we hear that there may be some opportunities in an organisation we know we should follow this up. Problem is, most cold calls just don't work. What you need is some way to turn a cold call into something else – if not a hot call, then at least a warm call. Well, the Web has made this possible. It takes is a bit of work and planning, but it can happen.

Never make cold calls – ever

The very best call you can make is one along the lines of, 'Jim asked me to call you'. The prospect knows and admires Jim; you are recommended; you get work. Sadly, those 'Jim asked me to call' routines are few and far between for many of us. So how do you get that all-important foot in the door?

As you may already have worked out, I hate cold calls. In fact, I just don't make them. Now if you are going to turn your back on them too, you need an effective substitute. At the risk of unleashing thousands of independent consultants feverishly calling punters, here's the way to do it.

You need a legitimate reason to call.

I can hear you saying it now, 'Oh *that's* clever!' Well, yes it is. What you are required to do is be able to engage someone in a conversation. That is all you need. You see, you don't sell anything. All you are going to do is pander to someone's curiosity and flatter their ego a little. Strangely enough, everyone likes that.

The 'legitimate' reason to call (the excuse) has to be just that – *real*. Well, it has to be real for me at least, because I am not very good at stretching truths (otherwise I would be a very rich conservatory or kitchen makeover salesperson). What I created some time ago was the research-led enquiry line. Basically, what you do is devise a piece of business-related research (which you will publish), and use that as your door opener.

As you can imagine, this works much better if you are carrying out research for some easily recognisable organisation or institution. So, one of the ways to make this work really well, is to get into bed with an organisation or institution (on a no-fee basis if necessary) and volunteer your services.

In my own case I have been pretty lucky, because I have become associated with a lot of research initiatives over the years, so I have already achieved a certain level of credibility. I have also published a lot (and have the evidence on my website to prove it).

But my suggestion to you is to start small and work your way up. For example, if you are working in a small community, develop and then create a study for your local chamber of commerce or similar group. This will allow you to visit members at their places of work. At the end of the study you self-publish (if necessary) and then organise a seminar or workshop on the findings. You can do this at any level: all you need is the great idea that will catch a person's interest.

I have even done this for clients who were seeking to expand their business horizons. What we did was tie up with a publisher and then carry out and publish a series of research papers, launching them with a roadshow of seminars. Most times, when you call a 'target' they are only too happy to oblige. The total legitimacy of the action comes, of course, at the end, when you send them a copy of the report or book you have completed.

Book yourself in

Writing a book that reinforces your professional expertise is another way of getting to meet new business prospects. In all these cases you end up with a hard-copy report (or similar) that becomes your current 'brochure.' And this will sell you a lot better than any glossy piece you can come up with yourself. By getting published, you are being legitimised by others. That is a pretty powerful statement.

Excuses to stay in touch

Of course, you can't always be writing a book or researching some emerging business issue (people will wonder if you ever do any real work!). So you have to create other reasons to stay in contact with those prospects you met. In this, I find that a newsletter, short on sell and big on content, works very well indeed – although only when it begins to appear on a regular basis (my view is that it takes four issues before anyone comes to accept it). Newsletters are not expensive to produce and print (less than a brochure!), and creating four issues a year is a basic minimum.

The type of newsletters I produce are in both hard copy and an electronic version, but it is the hard copy that gets read by clients and prospects (usually at home, on a train or in a plane!). Content is geared to their interests and is designed to provide a topical commentary on issues related to (in my case) communications, human resources, and the office of the future.

In my experience, newsletters more than pay for themselves. They give you some immediate recognition, but also act as a permanent reminder that you are always available to solve the problems you are warning them about.

Hot-topic seminars

Another way of staying in touch is to organise and run seminars on hot topics that you know will appeal to your prospect audience. These days the competition to mount these sorts of events is increasing, so it isn't easy to get a good turnout unless the subject is really compelling. All the same, it is worth trying to make this happen, as you then have a captive audience (who always appreciate *not* being sold to). Remember, know from the outset what you want to achieve. Don't invite too many people. If you are on your own, six or seven is the maximum if you want to achieve a lot of interaction and a lot of opportunity to talk with your audience. The setting and the hospitality don't need to be lavish – just appropriate.

Platform marketing: conferences and seminars

Getting invited to speak at conferences and seminars is another way to get across your ideas and what your business is offering. But make sure that you are going to generate the right amount of publicity for yourself and your services. Too many conference organisers seek to limit the commercial exposure you can have. If that is the case, it may not be worth actually doing the session. Also, carefully check out the reputation of the organisers and make certain they are a legitimate operator – not all of them are.

Samples and show reels

As I mentioned earlier, samples are great. The reason I write books is for the marketing value, not the sales. The reason I research and produce investigative reports is to gain access to new opportunities. So do a deal to get free or deeply discounted copies of any work from the publisher before you sign the contract.

In addition, if you get an opportunity to be filmed during a presentation, make sure you get a copy (and the same applies with radio interviews). Then you can either use them as discreet mailers, or put them on your website. If you are attending a conference that is being recorded, ensure you get a copy of the film or audio tape afterwards.

Creating your own network

We discussed networks in detail in Chapter 1, suggesting that it wasn't a very wise move to start working for yourself if you didn't have some kind of effective network in place. The other option – especially once you are an established 'name' – is to create your own network. To give you an idea of how this can be done, let me explain how I created the FutureWork Forum (a group of like-minded, but non-competing independent consultants).

My initial plan was to have an information exchange between people I knew and respected who were in the same position as me. In the early days, it was a security blanket made up of people I could talk to and bounce ideas off. You may recall that in Chapter 1 we talked about the need for shoulders to cry on: FutureWork Forum was my personal, professional shoulder,

Then, after we had met a few times face-to-face, I began to realise the power of this group. Its depth of knowledge, time in the market, and eagerness to stay up-to-date was incredible. Indeed, we had not just a 'talking' shop but a 'doing' organisation. And while everyone was their own boss, there was an increasing sense of collectiveness. On that basis, Johnson & Associates and the other members (we are now 20 individuals) are now very much a part of the FutureWork Forum. We run workshops in cities all over Europe and beyond, we carry out research and we write about the future world of work.

And there are spin-offs. When I go and present to a client or a prospect, I carry 14 other people with me on my shoulder. All 20 are eager and available to help. When my clients ask, 'Where is your support?', I say it is everywhere and it is across the whole gamut of human issues in business. I am still a sole trader, but I am also much bigger than that. I outline my views on where this is all going for the independent consultant in Chapter 9; but suffice to say, having a network that is strong but non-invasive has improved my ability both to market (proving that even after 20 years there is still a lot to learn) and to meet my clients' emerging needs.

If you can't do it – teach it!

I have never believed the truth of this phrase. What I do believe though is that as independents we can make a huge contribution to others. We can give a lot of our expertise and our time to help make things better for others. Again, do this and your personal stock and your recognition level will increase. You don't have to think of it as a part of the marketing process if you don't want to. Just know that it is. For independents, everything you do is part of marketing yourself, even if you don't recognise it as such.

Charitable work

Into the list comes charitable work. If you can teach, coach, add up numbers or help to sell things, you are wanted somewhere, somehow. Many of us in our early years of struggling to establish ourselves have little time for this. But again, as I said above, this too is a type of marketing. Through the charitable work I have been involved in I have met two good clients, whom I would possibly never have come across if I had not been giving my time. What you need to understand is that opportunity for sole traders can appear at any time; it is recognising that opportunity and acting on it that is the mark of the true independent professional.

Gifts to go

Finally, a silly subject to end this chapter with – gifts. Someone asked me, 'What do you do about gifts to your clients and prospects?' Answer? Nothing. I cannot see that pens, miniature radios, talking calendars and so on have anything to do with my business or my ability to get more. Sure, I take my clients out to dinner from time to time, but basically it is all down to making sure you do a good job – that, I believe, is what clients really appreciate and expect. Oh, and I'll send them a copy of my latest book or research report, which I would like to think adds to their education. Of course, there are some people who see giving as an intrinsic part of how they do business (see 'It's a wicker, wicker world out there' below). But it isn't for me, and I don't see that it has any real place in the marketing of professional services. Most likely, if I did start doling out gifts my clients would hint at the fact I was getting too successful and making too much money!

Don't forget in all this that you are marketing yourself. You are the product, you are what the client buys. So, at present, the only person you can let down is yourself. Now let's move on to Counting the Cost and see what it is really going to take to become the sole trader you've always wanted to be.

It's a wicker, wicker world out there

I have a pal of mine who is a civil engineering consultant. While that may sound grand, he has always played it very low-key. There are no glorious suspension bridges or motorways in his body of work, but there are a lot of cycle tracks, woodland walks, public toilets (including those special areas for dogs) and children's play areas. He is largely an unsung professional, going about his work quietly and without any fuss. While others seek stardom and reputation enhancement, he is happy with a 20-mile fence to plan.

One day I asked him, 'How do you market yourself?'

'Well, I don't suppose I do,' he replied. 'Never thought about it.'

'But how do you get your business?' I asked. 'Do you apply for tenders and stuff like that?' (I knew that most of his work was in the local public sector.)

'Oh no, I don't do that. Well, I don't need to. The hampers seem to take care of it.'

'What hampers?' I asked.

'The ones that I give to the ladies who schedule the work at the council offices,' he said. 'You see I used to buy them from Harrods' catalogue, but they got really expensive. So now I just buy 20 large wicker hampers and fill them myself.'

My friend ensures that each year the ladies who get the work distributed after it has been agreed by the local council get a hamper (and by now, after more than 10 years, they expect them). There are NO favours. All that happens is that the work assigned to my pal, somehow, miraculously rises through the order pile to the very top! Now that's marketing!

Key learning points

- Make your website your showroom.
- Find excuses for making calls. Never be forced into a completely cold call – they seldom work and make you look desperate.
- Create your own network, but remember it is variety you need, not people in exactly the same business as you!

Chapter 6

Counting the cost
(and the profit)

Where there is income tax, the just man will pay more and
the unjust less on the same amount of income.   *Plato*

Income tax has made more liars out of people than golf and
fishing have.   *Anonymous*

Possibly we should title this chapter 'The Responsible Independent
Consultant', because whether we like it or not, we have to ensure that we pay
our taxes and the rest. This has always been an area of doing business that I
have preferred to leave to others a lot more qualified than me, on the basis that
they are going to do it not only better, but probably a lot cheaper at the end
of the day. My personal advice on this is to get the best advice you can afford;
and remember, if it looks really cheap that is what you will get – cheap advice.

Taking my own advice, I am happy – not to say ecstatic – to turn this
chapter over to my own accountant Peter Clegg, a partner of Westlake Clark
in New Milton, Hampshire (www.westlakeclark.com). If you have any questions on this section be sure to e-mail him – he knows what he is doing.

Peter has asked me to make it clear that we have used UK examples
throughout this chapter. Obviously laws, rules, regulations and local practices differ from country to country. If in doubt, call a good accountant!

*Note: All the information and examples used in this chapter were correct to May,
2005. Examples are used as a guide only.*

What do you need to make?

This is a crucial question. You need to make enough to pay your taxes and
your household bills and to provide for you and your family. So, to make ends
meet you need to look at your pricing model.

Here is an example.

	£	£
Sales/fees		79,000
(8 hours a day for 192 days at an hourly rate of £51)		
Direct costs		
Salaries	−4,700	
Advertising	−4,000	
Travel and subsistence	−3,300	
		(12,000)
		67,000
Overheads		
Telephone and fax	−2,000	
Motor expenses	−2,100	
Stationery and postage	−900	
		(5,000)
Profit before tax (PBT)		62,000
Taxation		(12,000)
Post tax profit (or what is left over for you)		50,000

Based on not unreasonable figures, this example shows that you need to earn £51 per hour over 192 8-hour days in order to end up with net income, post tax, of £50,000 p.a.

However, do not forget that you will need to spend some non-billable time on networking and prospecting for work. You may need to allocate some 20 per cent of your time for these tasks, meaning that the remaining 80 per cent of your time must generate revenue. Hence, this example only shows 192 income generating days, the balance being non-fee earning time that is devoted to marketing and prospecting for work.

You do not have to charge on an hourly basis, but you have to have a good idea of how long each assignment will take in order to get your pricing right. And if you think that £51 per hour seems expensive, think of what your garage or your plumber charges – not to mention your accountant or your solicitor!

What sort of business should you be?

Am I a sole trader or limited company? How do I function as an indie? How do networks and partnerships work?

As an independent in the UK, you have two real options:

- You can be self-employed as a sole proprietor or sole trader.
- You can run your business through a limited company.
  So what are the advantages, disadvantages and key features of each?

Sole trader

Advantages

- Confidentiality – virtually no information is available about you in the public domain unless you want to put it there.
- Freedom to manoeuvre, with very little regulation.
- Easy to operate.
- Easy to start and easy to finish.
- You pay tax each year on your profits as you earn them.

Disadvantages

- Unlimited liability – if anything goes wrong, apart from any insurance cover that you may have (for public or employers liability or indemnity insurance), you are totally and personally liable for any claims that are made against you.
- Tax planning is difficult, as you pay tax on the profits as you earn them.
- Higher taxes than using a limited company.

Limited company

Advantages

- Easy to establish – you can buy or form a ready-made limited company for around £60 or less, if you shop around.
- Limited liability for the shareholders, so most litigation should stop with the company, protecting the directors and shareholders.
- Tax planning can be easier.
- More tax efficient than the sole trader option.

Disadvantages

- Some financial information needs to be on file in the public domain, principally at Companies House where abbreviated annual accounts need to be filed, together with details of the company's directors, company secretary and shareholders.

- Higher administrative burden than being a sole trader, but, on balance, not that much worse. For example, a limited company will need to operate a PAYE scheme for just you as a director.

A limited company must have at least one shareholder, together with at least one director assisted by a company secretary. If you only have one director, this person cannot also be the company secretary. Ask your spouse or partner to be your company secretary if this is the case.

Any other thoughts here? Well, if you are starting off as an independent in a small way and want to test the water, then working as a sole trader is a cheap and inexpensive option, as you can, relatively painlessly, always convert your sole trading business to a limited company later on with very little tax downside. However, do not underestimate the importance of limited liability. Some of your clients, customers and suppliers may be vexatious litigants, and using a limited company gives you a considerable element of protection from their depravations (plus a certain amount of kudos and status). In addition, to some clients you will always look more attractive as a limited company (however small) than as a sole trader. (See Appendix 1 for some comparisons of the tax and accounting policy of these two options.)

What about networks and partnerships?

Here again there are contrasts.

Networks

A network is a group of like-minded individual sole traders or limited companies who work together on an informal basis by sharing work, contacts and resources. Crucially, however, each member of the group is likely to be 'independent', and so running his or her own individual business. The network is a mini trade association. So, in getting involved in a network there are some points to watch:

- Where does legal liability for any mistakes lie?
- Who is entitled to revenues and profits from a particular assignment?
- How do you share costs, including common costs such as websites, advertising and marketing?
- What happens when one of your network members runs off with your best client?
- How do you police your network? Can the bad behaviour of one member drag you all down?

All of these difficult concepts are best dealt with by all members of the network agreeing on a clear set of rules at the outset.

Partnership

Partnership involves two or more individuals carrying on business together to generate profits (a legal definition that has so far survived unchanged from the Partnership Act 1890). Partners in a business have joint and several liability for all of the liabilities and obligations of the partnership. This means that if the partnership has unpaid bills and Partner A cannot pay, then Partner B is liable for all of the partnership's obligations.

Here are some important features of partnerships:

- In tax law, a partnership is taxed in the same way as a sole trader would be, except that there are two or more individuals involved.
- A partnership agreement setting out the obligations and responsibilities of the partners to each other is a must. Otherwise the partnership is governed under the rules contained in the Partnership Act 1890.
- Taking this a stage further, your partnership could trade as a limited company, with each 'partner' being a director and shareholder in the limited company.
- As an alternative you could set up an LLP (Limited Liability Partnership), which is an ordinary partnership from a tax perspective, but gives the individual partners limited liability, with the trade-off being the need to file financial information and accounts at Companies House.

Getting in the professionals

What do accountants, solicitors, bookkeepers and the bank manager do for you (keep you out of trouble with the taxman for one thing!), and how do you go about finding them?

Leaving aside the school of thought that none of these people in suits can ever help you, I subscribe to the view of getting professional help unless you are in the business yourself, and not wasting time on reading the instructions unless you have to. So here is a brief guide to these back room supporters. But do remember that none of these individuals will make your business a success or a failure. That is down to you.

Accountants

Most accountants will have a professional qualification (eg, be a member of one of the professional bodies – see Appendix 4 for details). They should help you decide on the most appropriate structure for you, that is, whether to be sole trader or limited company or partnership. Accountants are there to guide you through the taxation and administrative red tape of running your business so that you keep on the right side of the tax man, know what profit you can keep, pay your taxes on time and steer clear of trouble.

How do you find an accountant? The most reliable method is by word of mouth. Listen to recommendations and testimonials from friends and colleagues. Talk to two or three accountants to see what they can offer you and whether you gel with them on a personal basis. Ideally, you probably do not need an accountant who is working with an organisation that dwarfs yours in size – you need someone who is used to working with the problems that you will encounter. Find out what the prices will be for the various items of work that you need done. Identify how any extras or odd services will be priced. Most accountants will charge you on an hourly basis and will give you a fairly good quotation for what your basic work needs will be. But, just like getting building work done at home, consider whether you will want any extras or whether you will want to vary the work specified, as this will invariably lead to extra cost. Talk through the time-frame for providing information to your accountant, and be clear as to where the responsibilities lie.

Finally, remember that your accountant should be enabling and empowering you to see your way through the regulatory and taxation framework, and his advice could save you considerable amounts of tax, time and frustration

Legal support and solicitors

You will need a solicitor for those moments when you have a contractual dispute with a customer or supplier, are entering into a network or joint venture agreement, or have issues to clarify on employment law, ranging from employment contracts all the way through to issues that might involve you being taken to an employment tribunal. Because high street solicitors tend to work mainly in the areas of conveyancing, matrimonial, wills and probate, make sure that the solicitor you choose can offer you support in business related areas. Generally, the bigger the legal practice, the more specialisation is available in the areas that you may need as an independent; but with this specialisation comes higher cost and the need for you to deal with a bigger legal firm.

Solicitors are also best chosen by recommendation and by looking for a firm which matches your needs and philosophy. A useful starting point is the Law Society website: www.lawsociety.org.uk.

Bookkeepers

If you do not want to run your own accounting support package to keep your daily books and records, you may want a bookkeeper to do this for you. Bookkeepers are much cheaper than accountants and will be able to offer you the one or two days per month or per quarter that you need to keep your records in order. In early 2005, they cost anywhere between £8 to £30 per hour, depending on where you are located and on their skill and quality. You must be prepared to pay the market rate to get the work done properly and efficiently. Again, word of mouth is quite helpful, and your accountant will be able to point you in the right direction of a suitable bookkeeper.

Bank managers

You will need (and sooner rather than later) a separate bank account for your business receipts and payments. In any case, running the business as a limited company does, of necessity, require a bank account opened in the name of the limited company. Only if you are starting life as an independent as a sole trader on a small-scale basis can you really get along by continuing to use your own personal bank account.

So what are the ins and outs of business banking?

- When choosing a bank, you can either use the same bank that provides your current personal checking account or mortgage or, for diversity, set up a relationship with a different banking provider.
- There will be bank charges for pay-ins and withdrawals (although most of the large banks will not make any charges for at least the first 12 months).
- The days of an individual bank manager being a semi-permanent fixture within your chosen branch have gone. You have to be prepared for the individual with whom you establish a relationship moving on sooner rather than later. Therefore, you need to choose your business bank based on the services it offers, such as free accounting packages and introductory 'free' banking periods.
- You may want a business charge card on your business bank account.
- If you want to borrow money for the business, you will find that the bank will want to put in place some form of security for this lending (such as a second mortgage on your home), to charge an arrangement fee, and to charge you interest for the privilege.
- Unsecured lending is usually only possible for relatively small amounts of borrowing, although you can explore the Department of Trade and Industry (DTI) sponsored loan guarantee scheme.

- Secured lending will mean that if the business does collapse, you are still liable to the bank even if you are trading as a limited company.
- Do tell your bank what is going on regularly. Send them copies of your annual accounts. This helps you to keep in touch and maintain a relationship.
- Do not go overdrawn without first discussing this with the bank – it makes it so much easier if you have been in touch beforehand.

Contracts with clients

Do not work for free unless this is your choice. Make it clear up front to your clients what your terms of business are, when you will invoice them and when you expect to get paid. Set this out in an exchange of letters (preferably) or e-mails with your supplier, so that you are creating a binding understanding or contract between you.

Make sure that your invoicing refers to the original contract. If you do not get paid, you may need to consider stopping work for your client. Try not to be fobbed off by excuses about cash flow difficulties on their side – after all, if they are paying their own staff every month why should they not pay you too? If you are still having trouble, consider taking legal advice – and if the contract you are setting up in the first place strikes you as complicated, take legal advice at this stage as well. This is where your solicitor can really help you.

Contracts with suppliers

Whatever you are buying in for your business, try to find out what this will cost and when you need to pay for it before you buy it. What payment terms do your suppliers require? Some items (such as travel or life insurance) have to be paid more or less instantly, while other providers may give you at least 30 days' credit.

Try to agree similar contract terms or issues with your suppliers as you would with your own clients or customers.

The taxman cometh

Just what are your legal obligations to the tax man, what can you claim for and how can you minimise your tax obligations?

To set the scene here, your obligations and what you can claim for will differ slightly depending on whether you are a sole trader or a limited company. The taxes you have to deal with are administered by Her Majesty's Revenue and Customs (HMRC) (responsible for national insurance and direct taxation) and indirect taxation (principally VAT, as far as you're concerned). HMRC was formed in Spring 2005 as a result of a merger between the Inland Revenue and HM Customs and Excise.

You have three significant tax areas to keep under control.

VAT (Value Added Tax)

This is a tax on goods and services, and so applies to the services that you will supply as an independent. It is a sales (or turnover) based tax and will be levied on you regardless of your profitability. Your liability to be involved with VAT depends on whether your sales (commonly called turnover) exceed £58,000 p.a. Above this level of sales (or turnover) you have to register for VAT compulsorily. Below this limit you can register on a voluntary basis, which can be a good idea if your clients are VAT-registered because they can recover the input VAT that you charge them. This means that financially you will be better off, because you can reclaim input VAT on any supplies (subject to VAT) that you buy in.

The current main rate of VAT is 17.5 per cent. Most supplies or services provided by independents will be subject to VAT at this standard rate, but there can be exceptions – such as for work done overseas, for example – for which the VAT rate could be zero. However, if in doubt, be prepared to charge VAT at the standard rate and make sure (obtaining written advice from your accountant or HMRC) that it is appropriate to charge any of your services at a rate other than 17.5 per cent. Remember that VAT is a self-assessing tax, and you will be liable for any mistakes.

You normally pay over any VAT that you have charged on your sales revenue (less any input VAT on allowable purchases) on a quarterly basis, and your quarterly VAT return needs to be filed with HMRC within one month of each quarter end. If you miss this deadline for filing your VAT return and making payment you will be penalised.

There are certain helpful schemes run by HMRC to help independents, including:

- A flat-rate VAT scheme for businesses with a sales turnover of up to £150,000 p.a.
- An accounting scheme that is annual as an alternative to filing your VAT returns quarterly (although you will pay VAT on a [more or less] monthly basis, based on an estimate of your annual VAT due).
- You can report your VAT due based on sales revenue banked and supplies paid for (commonly called a 'cash accounting' basis), which means that

you only have to pay over VAT after your clients have paid you (this is good for cash flow planning)

- A brief summary of the supplies and purchases on which you can reclaim input VAT is included later on in this chapter (see pp. 117–18).
- Above all, failing to register for VAT when you need to (because your sales turnover for the previous twelve months has exceeded £58,000) can cause you significant financial penalties and difficulties.
- Something that you may find strange about VAT is that if (say) you are a sole trader, your VAT registration encompasses all business activities carried on by you personally, not just those that you carry out as an 'independent'. So if, for example, you carry out some freelance paid writing as a sideline activity and you are also an independent sole trader, then both activities are aggregated for the purposes of deciding whether you should register for VAT compulsorily, and also for working out your VAT each quarter, so that you would have to charge VAT on your freelance writing activities.
- Finally, as with so many things in life, as VAT is a transaction-based tax, take advice before the transactions occur: speak to your accountant or bookkeeper or the HMRC helpline and get it right first time.

National insurance

The contributory-based principles of the post war 'Beveridge' era are now well in the past, and national insurance – administered by the HMRC – is now becoming, more and more, an earnings and payroll tax that has increasingly little bearing on any state retirement pension you will receive. There are different classes of national insurance contribution (NIC):

Class 1 – payable by both employers and employees
Class 2 – payable by sole traders
Class 3 – voluntary contributions (which we will ignore)
Class 4 – payable by sole traders
and
Class 1A – paid by employers only on taxable benefits provided to staff.

It is helpful to split national insurance obligations between sole traders and limited companies at this point.

Sole traders

- Class 2 NIC. This is a flat-rate contribution paid at £2.10 per week. You should notify to pay this within three months of starting sole trading self-employment, otherwise there is a £100 fixed penalty. Paying approximately

£107 p.a. qualifies you with contributions towards the basic state pension at retirement age (currently worth around £80 per week).

- Class 4 NIC. These are profit-related contributions and are payable, along with your self-assessment income tax bill, at the following rates:

£0 to £4,895	0%
£4,896 to £32,760	8%
£32,761 upwards	1%

Limited companies

Within a limited company, Class 1 NIC is payable by both employers and employees on earnings at the following rates:

Employers

£0 to £4,895	0%
£4,896 upwards	12.8%

Employees

£0 to £4,895	0%	
£4,896 to £32,760	11%	(maximum £3,065)
£32,761 upwards	1%	

As you can see, national insurance contributions for any employer can be very expensive, with the employer contributions currently standing at 12.8 per cent of salary.

For this reason, the choice of sole trader status or limited company status and the method of extracting profit from your limited company is something that you should discuss in detail with your accountant.

Class 1A NIC

This is payable by employers only, and stands at 12.8 per cent on taxable benefits in kind provided to staff (and directors, if a limited company). It is payable by 19 July each year for the tax year ended on the previous 5 April.

Corporation tax and income tax (and other direct taxes, such as capital gains tax)

This area of taxation is also administered by the HMRC.

You will only come into contact with *corporation tax* if you trade through a limited company. The rate at which it is payable is usually – for an independent – around 19 per cent of the profit made by the company in each year, and any corporation tax is usually payable nine months after the end of the company's financial year end.

While you may hear that the first £10,000 of profits are not subject to corporation tax, this will not be the case if you take dividends from your limited company: the corporation tax rate will then be much closer to 19 per cent. This is a good topic for you to discuss with your accountant or, if you have the time, to check out on the HMRC's website (www.hmrc.gov.uk). You will also find a worked example at Appendix 1.

Income tax will affect you whether you are a sole trade or a limited company. As a sole trader it will be paid – twice per annum – on 31 January and 31 July (together with any Class 4 NICs), based on the profits made in your business in the tax year. The rates at which it is payable (ignoring any other income) are as follows:

£0 to £4,895	0%	(this is the 'personal allowance')
£4,896 to £6,985	10%	
£6,986 to £37,295	22%	
£37,296 upwards	40%	

Using a limited company, income tax is payable on the salary or dividends that you withdraw. For salary payments, income tax (along with national insurance) should be deducted from your monthly salary payments under the PAYE system, in the same way that it was for you by your previous employer before you became an independent. The only difference is that you, as a director of your limited company, are responsible for operating PAYE. So among your other new administrative duties, you are now payroll manager!

What can I claim for?

So, armed with this basic outline, what can you claim for and how can you minimise your tax obligations?

An overview of some of the common claimable and non-claimable costs reads like this:

	Limited company		Sole trader	
	Tax	VAT	Tax	VAT
Your own salary	Yes	No	No	No
Working spouse/partner's salary	Yes	No	Yes	No
Business motor expenses				
Petrol	Yes	Yes	Yes	Yes
Road Tax	Yes	No	Part	No
Insurance	Yes	No	Yes	No
Repairs	Yes	Yes	Yes	Yes
Depreciation	Part	No	Part	No
Finance charges	Yes	No	Part	No

		Limited company		Sole trader	
		Tax	VAT	Tax	VAT
Travel					
Taxis		Yes	V	Yes	V
Train		Yes	No	Yes	No
Air fares		Yes	No	Yes	No
Hotels		Yes	Yes	Yes	Yes
Meals (but not entertaining)		Yes	Yes	Yes	Yes
Telephone and fax		Yes	Yes	Yes	Yes
Mobile phone		Yes	Yes	Yes	Yes
IT costs		Yes	Yes	Yes	Yes
Home costs					
Light and heat		Part	No	Part	No
Repairs		Part	No	Part	No
Insurance		Part	No	Part	No
Stationery		Yes	Yes	Yes	Yes
Postage		Yes	No	Yes	No
Advertising		Yes	Yes	Yes	Yes
Insurance					
Equipment		Yes	No	Yes	No
Public/employer's liability		Yes	No	Yes	No
Personal	BIK	Yes	No	No	No
Entertaining		No	No	No	No
Interest on bank loans		Yes	No	Yes	No
Bank charges		Yes	No	Yes	No
Pensions and life assurance					
Life assurance		No	No	No	No
Income protection		No	No	No	No
Medical insurance	BIK	Yes	No	No	No
Mortgage protection	BIK	Yes	No	No	No
Earnings protection	BIK	Yes	No	No	No
Pension contributions		Yes	No	TD	No	No

Key:

V = depends on whether the supplier is VAT registered

BIK = creates a taxable benefit in kind for the employee

TD = basic rate tax credit given at source by the HMRC (for individuals)

This is not an exhaustive guide and is included to provide illumination rather than support, but should give you a feel for what you can and cannot do. Above all, for VAT, income tax and corporation tax purposes you do need to keep records and receipts for all expenditure for which you want to claim.

Calculating and minimising your tax

So, let us assume that you are billing fees of £80,000 to your clients, and that after deducting various costs you are left with a profit of £50,000. Your tax position, using the 2005/2006 tax year, would be:

Sole trader: £14,470 tax and NIC payable

Limited company paying out full salary: £15,590 tax and NIC payable

Limited company paying out a low salary but some dividends: £10,505 tax and NIC payable

As you can see, your choice as to whether you are a sole trader or limited company can have profound tax implications. So, talk to your accountant and weigh up the pros and cons.

But do be aware that the tax picture will change from year to year, and what is good this year may not be so good next year. Here are some current 'hot' issues in tax:

'IR35'

If you are operating as an independent through a limited company and any of your contracts with your clients could be construed as being of an 'employer and employee' nature, if your limited company was hypothetically stripped away, then you would need to take out most of your remuneration from your limited company by means of salary rather than dividends, which means that your tax position could be rather worse than operating as a sole trader. 'IR35' is the name and style given to the March 1999 Inland Revenue press release that announced this legislation, which is intended to prevent tax avoidance. It is an ongoing and contentious piece of legislation, about which books have been written in their own right. For example, Anne Redston has already reached the second edition of her book *IR35: Personal Service Companies,* running to some 550 pages.

Useful information on this subject is also available from the Professional Contractors group website at www.pcg.org.uk. A very brief guide to how this legislation works is set out in Appendix 2.

Paying dividends rather than salary through your limited company

As we've already seen, paying dividends is currently better than paying salary. But against a backdrop of a growing government budget deficit, tax rises may occur in spring 2006, and the advantage of trading through a limited company and following the low salary/high dividend route may be further eroded as a result.

The pros and cons of paying your partner or spouse salary as opposed to dividends are explored in more detail further on in this chapter.

Working tax credits and child tax credits

Your level of income, combined with that of your spouse or partner, will impact on the level of any child tax credit or working tax credit award that you receive from the Inland Revenue. So, apart from considering the headline rate of tax, do not forget to consider any means tested awards you receive.

Child tax credits and working tax credits generally depend on the combined joint incomes of both you and your spouse or partner in any tax year. They can be a valuable source of support in your early years as an independent.

Remember that you cannot backdate a claim for these benefits, so you must file and claim for your entitlement early in each tax year (preferably before 5 July for a tax year beginning on the previous 6 April) for at least a provisional award, which is then finally adjusted after the end of the tax year (the following 5 April), when final details of your joint incomes will be known.

So if you miss out on submitting your claim for a provisional award, then no claim can be backdated by more than three months. The lowest level of claim awardable, of around £545 p.a. (for a person or couple with children), will be restricted and clawed back once your joint total exceeds £54,000 p.a.

Your legal obligations to the tax man

Each year, whether you are a sole trader or a limited company, you will have to file various sorts of tax returns with the HMRC (and, if you operate as a limited company, with Companies House as well). Most of these forms, returns and obligations are dealt with later (see pp. 130–131).

Most importantly, both sole traders and limited companies must submit their accounts annually to the Inland Revenue.

You must also keep records of your revenues and costs, substantiated, as far as possible, by keeping receipts, copy invoices and bank statements. Also, these records should regularly be processed – this is particularly important for a limited company, which has an additional legal duty under the Companies Act 1985 to maintain regular accounting records

Getting a bank manager you can work with? Is that possible?

Undoubtedly you can find a bank that you can work with, but finding a bank manager with whom you will always have a good relationship may be difficult to start with. Bank managers (or business bankers as they may be known) are always anxious for promotion and advancement. You must expect that your business manager within your bank is going to move on.

To get the best out of your bank you must work at maintaining the relationship. Provide information on a regular quarterly or six-monthly basis so that your bank manager knows what you are up to. I would recommend that you send profit-and-loss accounts and balance sheets, together with any cash flow forecasts that you might prepare.

Banks – just like you – do not like surprises. So if there is a difficult tax bill approaching that needs to be paid, talk to your bank manager in good time. Do not phone him the night before the cheque is about to clear!

Recognise that your bank manager is not an independent. You must realise that he is still in that comfort zone of full-time employment with a salary cheque coming in every month!

You need a loan like a hole in the head

Loans will cost you money, not only in interest charges but also in arrangement fees. Planning your cash flow (and most bank introductory packs contain a proforma) should help you to ensure that your bank balance stays in credit and avoid you having to take a loan in the first place.

Agreeing regular invoicing or billing patterns with your clients is important. You will find that working with clients who are larger than you – an inevitable consequence as an independent – means you are dealing with large organisations that will pay on credit terms or 30 or 60 days. Getting your invoicing done on time is important, as is making sure that this matches the payment authorisation programmes of your suppliers as well.

If you do this and yet still need a loan, it is probably only because you are not managing your own cash flow positively. Think and plan ahead, and use your bookkeeper or accountant to help you develop planning strategies if you need to.

Supplies, supplies, supplies

Here it pays, as always, to shop around and use the Internet to seek out the best deals; but do heed the advice given previously and agree the terms of business with all your suppliers.

Don't forget though that while it may be cheaper to buy some services and supplies on-line, from time to time you may need a more personal service. A local insurance broker or IT hardware engineer, used to dealing with unusual requests, may give you more immediate and relevant service.

Pension plan contributions

This is certainly not a must-have early on in your independent business, but you should review your needs carefully once you are established. You should, particularly, take detailed independent financial advice on the relevance and investment performance of any past pension entitlement that you may have built up.

State retirement pension entitlement

This, although you may not realise it, is a benefit that can be bought quite cheaply. Paying either £2.10 per week in Class 2 NIC as a sole trader, or taking a modest level of salary from your limited company (as low as £82 per week) will help you to maintain you entitlement to a full basic state pension, which is currently worth around £80 per week on retirement.

Hiring staff and subcontract help

Set out right from the start what the rules of engagement are, including how much you have to pay and when. Although it is cheaper – particularly from a tax perspective – to hire subcontract or freelance/self-employed assistance, it is the facts of the work actually done that determines whether it is employment or self-employment. If you are hiring staff on an employed basis, not only do you have to deal with employment legislation (including that concerned with paid holidays, sick pay and other employment law issues), but you must operate the deduction of income tax and employee national insurance from any salary paid and you must also pay employer's national insurance on top of this. Therefore, if you are hiring staff you need to budget for an extra 12.8 per cent for employers national insurance contributions.

HMRC will expect you to get the employee/self-employed distinction correct, and if any self-employed consultants or freelancers are subsequently reclassified as employees by HMRC then you, and not your self-employed consultants or freelancers, will be liable for any PAYE and NIC deductions that should have been made, together with penalties and interest.

Accounting packages, domain names and other sources of support

There are some good entry-level accounting packages for the independent, such as:

- Sage instant
- Taz books
- Quicken.

All of these can help to make your accounting life less stressful.

While forming a limited company can help, in a small way, to protect your business name, you should also consider securing the domain name for your business website.

You might also want to register a trademark and other intellectual property rights if these are a significant asset to your business, and you would be susceptible to competitive infringement in these areas.

Finally, do not underestimate the help you can obtain, (both free of charge and subsidised), by using the DTI-sponsored business link service (www. businesslink.gov.uk). Attending their events can also provide very helpful networking opportunities

Working from home claims

If you are working from home, then any extra household costs involved in running your office can be claimed for, including:

- additional light and heat costs
- business furniture
- telephone, fax and Internet costs
- additional insurance.

All of these costs can usually be claimed by means of a round sum adjustment called 'use of home as office', which can range from £5 per week upwards depending on actual circumstance – but do not overclaim, as HMRC will scale back any unreasonable claims. For sole traders, a reasonable (in the view of HMRC, not you!) business-use related portion of your home mortgage interest can also be claimed.

Remember though that if you are claiming a fixed proportion of your home costs against tax then part of your home can become an asset for capital gains tax purposes when you sell your home, so consider any claims that you make with care.

Travel – the unromantic stuff you need to know

As an independent you are likely to run your business from home. Therefore, most of your travel costs will be tax deductible, whether for train, car, plane or taxi. Do keep records and all the receipts, as you will need these to substantiate any business expenses. Having said this, if you are working on a long project with one client and are based at their offices, it is possible that your place of business for tax purposes may become your client's premises, so that your home to work travel is effectively commuting and, therefore, the costs are not tax deductible any longer. For a more in-depth discussion of this topic, look at HMRC's booklet, which can be accessed at the following website addresses: www.hmrc.gov.uk/guidance/480.pdf; www.hmrc.gov.uk/helpsheets/490.pdf.

Family and the independent consultant

Leaving aside the taxation issues, you need to think through the emotional issues of working during the day with your partner, whom you have probably only seen outside working hours for the last few years. Just for starters, think about those music stars who have been unable to cope with being together in the same band as well as having a long term relationship.

Thinking now of the tax issues, yes, you can pay your spouse or partner to work in your business. The golden rules are:

- The payments must actually be made by cheque or by cash.
- What you pay should be justified in terms of the duties carried out.
- What you pay should be in line with the national minimum wage.

Make sure that what you pay is not excessive compared to your spouse's actual input and, by inference, not tax driven. Otherwise any excess remuneration could then be reassessed on you if you are challenged by HMRC, leaving you liable to higher tax charges that you might not be anticipating.

Does your spouse or partner need a contract of employment? Definitely a question for your solicitor! I am sure that the theoretical answer is yes, but the practical, real world answer might be no.

As an alternative to employment, you may wish your spouse/partner to be either a 'partner' in your sole trading business or a shareholder in your limited company. In this way, you could reduce the tax that you pay at higher rates by using up your spouse/partner's unused basic rate (22 per cent) tax band. HMRC are all too aware of this ploy, and if your spouse or partner is not fully contributing to the business profits then their profit share or dividends could be reassessed on you, negating any tax advantage. This planning strategy attacked in 'Arctic Systems' tax case, together with the 'IR35' issue, are the two most contentious independent tax issues currently in play.

Finally, can you pay your children? The strict answer is no, both for tax and employment law reasons. However, by the time your children have reached their early to mid-teens, paying modest sums for real business tasks performed (such as envelope stuffing and genuine administrative duties) is acceptable, although strictly you will need permission from your metropolitan or county council up until the age of 16 to do so – otherwise you will be breaking the law.

Cars and other vehicles

Unfortunately, as you will discover, this merits its own (not too) small section!

To get one thing straight first, you will find that the tax system is pretty restrictive, focusing any tax deductions on the business use of your car, but also capable of delivering some unpleasant surprises!

VAT

You will not be able to reclaim any input VAT on the purchase of your car, nor will you have to charge any output VAT on sale, unless you are in the very unlikely scenario of making a profit (selling price less purchase cost) on sale.

You can, however, reclaim input VAT on:

- repairs and maintenance costs
- fuel costs: but for business mileage only, and therefore subject to an adjustment for private usage if you reclaim input VAT on all (ie both business and private) of your car fuel costs
- 50 per cent of the input VAT on any contract hire or operating lease costs (an arrangement by which you do not own the vehicle, but hire it from a third party owner under an operating lease).

These VAT rules apply whether you are a sole trader or a limited company. For general taxation, however, the rules will differ depending on which status you claim.

Sole trader

What you can deduct and claim for will depend on accurately recording your business and private mileage each year. This is something that you will find rather irritating, but is has to be done! It is also an Inland Revenue requirement.

The concepts of what is deductible are best illustrated by a worked example, for which we will assume that in Year 1 you drive 18,000 miles, split as follows:

Business miles	10,800	60%
Private miles	7,200	40%
Total	18,000	100%

Your car (new to you) cost £15,000, financed by a hire purchase loan of £10,000, on which you pay interest of £800 in Year 1.

Your running costs for Year 1 are:

Road tax	£150
Insurance	£750
Repairs	£1,000
Fuel	£2,400
Total	£4,300

Your tax deductions can then be analysed like this:

Capital, depreciation and interest costs

- capital and depreciation

cost		£15,000
tax depreciation or capital allowances limited to the lower of 25% or £3,000		−£3,000
adjusted for private use	40%	−£1,200
tax claimable amount	60%	£1,800
tax value of car carried forward to Year 2		£12,000

- interest costs

interest paid		£800
interest disallowed		
$1/2$ of purchase cost in excess of £12,000		
$\dfrac{1/2 \times (15{,}000 - 12{,}000)}{15{,}000} \times 800$		−£160
allowable interest		£640
adjusted for private use	40%	−£256
tax claimable amount	60%	£384

- running costs

  These are pro-rated between business and private use

total running costs		£5,300
adjusted for private use	40%	−£2,120
tax claimable amount	60%	£3,180
Total deductions in 'year 1'		£5,364

An alternative concessionary method for sole traders, offered by HMRC if your sales turnover is less than the VAT turnover limit of £58,000, is to claim an overall deduction on a mileage basis, similar to that for employees, like this:

Business miles driven: 10,800

10,000 miles at	40p per mile	£4,000
800 miles at	25p per mile	£200
Total deductions in 'year 1'		£4,200

These mileage rates include all costs, including interest and depreciation and capital allowances, but the trade off is simplicity.

Limited company

Here there are two routes: either the company provides you with a company car, or you provide your own car, and your limited company reimburses you for your business motoring costs.

Company car for you

As a taxable benefit in kind, its value is based on a combination of the new list price of the car (not what you may have bought it for second-hand) and the car's CO_2 emission rating. So it works out at a minimum of 15 per cent of the new list price for a car with a low CO_2 emission rating, running to a top rate of 35 per cent of the new list price for a car with a high CO_2 rating.

Therefore, if your car has a new list price of £15,000 and an 'average' CO_2 rating of 190g of CO_2/km, then the benefit in kind would be:

£15,000 x 25% = £3,750

So you will pay income tax on the benefit of £3,750, at either 22 or 40 per cent, and the company will pay Class 1A NIC at 12.8 per cent (totalling £480 p.a.).

Fuel for private motoring is not usually a tax efficient benefit. The benefit for 2005/2006 would be £14,400 x 25% (the CO_2 emission %), and would involve an additional taxable benefit of £3,600. You would need to drive around 10,000 or more private miles each year for this to be tax efficient. So, your limited company should only pay for business mileage.

Any car or car fuel benefits are reported by the limited company on form P11D each year. You then report your taxable benefit on your personal tax return.

Company car for the limited company

If we are making the same assumptions as for a sole trader:

Capital, depreciation and interest costs

- capital and depreciation

cost		£15,000
tax depreciation or capital allowances limited to the lower of 25% or £3,000		−£3,000
adjusted for private use	0%	−nil
tax claimable amount	100%	£3,000
tax value of car carried forward to Year 2		£12,000

- interest costs

interest paid		£800
interest disallowed		
$1/2$ of purchase cost in excess of £12,000		
$\dfrac{1/2 \times (15{,}000 - 12{,}000)}{15{,}000} \times 800$		−£160
allowable interest		£640
adjusted for private use	0%	−nil
tax claimable amount	100%	£640

- running costs
  These are not pro-rated between business and private use

total running costs		
[excluding private fuel costs of £960]		£4,340
adjusted for private use	0%	−nil
tax claimable amount	100%	£4,340
Total deductions in Year 1		**£7,980**

Provide your own car

You can claim for your business mileage costs as above, so that if you drive 10,800 business miles in a year, then your limited company can reimburse you, tax free £4,200.

No other deductions are available and if your limited company reimburses you for, or pays for, motoring costs totalling more than £4,200, then this excess is subject to income tax and national insurance. So, for example, if you claim 70p per business mile from your limited company because you run a Jaguar, making the reimbursement £7,560, then the excess of £3,360 is taxable.

And finally, company vans or pick ups …

You might take a liking to using a 'double-cab pick up'! Would your clients like this too? Assuming yes on both counts, then your limited company can:

- reclaim input VAT on purchase
- claim full capital allowances of up to 40 per cent on purchase in Year 1, (without the £3,000 restriction that is in place for cars)
- claim all the running costs as tax deductible.

For you, as a director or member of staff, the benefit in kind is only £500 p.a. until April 2007, when the benefit in kind will increase to £3,000 p.a.

This is a pretty good deal, but do bear in mind that your double-cab pick up should have a payload capacity of over 1 tonne in order to qualify.

Dealing with deadlines

Finally, something that you are already used to, but with a difference ...

As either a sole trader or a limited company, you will have numerous extra deadlines to watch out for, apart from your normal 'work' related commitments!

Missing any of them is likely to cost you money in terms of penalties, extra tax and interest on extra tax.

Here are some of the more important deadlines:

Common deadlines for both sole traders and limited companies

- 19 of each month
  PAYE/NIC payable on payroll deductions made in the previous month (although as a 'small' employer you will most likely be able to opt to pay your PAYE/NIC over quarterly)

- 31 January
  1 File your personal tax return for the tax year ended on the previous 5 April.
  2 Pay personal tax due (final, third or balancing payment for the previous tax year + first instalment on account for the current tax year).

- 19 April
  Interest runs on any PAYE/NIC due but so far unpaid for the tax year ended on 5 April.

- 19 May
  File form P35 (end of tax year payroll return) with the Inland Revenue. Don't forget to give your staff their P60s too.

- 30 June
  File child tax credit and working tax credit claim forms,

- 6 July
  P11D forms to be filed, reporting benefits in kind for staff (and directors, if a limited company). Don't forget to give your staff a copy of their P11Ds too.

- 19 July
  Pay over any Class 1A NIC due on taxable benefits in kind.

- 31 July
  Pay personal tax due (second instalment on account for the tax year just finished).

- and finally, quarterly ...
  file your VAT returns and pay over any VAT due within one month of your VAT quarter end.

Sole traders only

- Within 3 months of starting as a sole trader
  Register to pay Class 2 NIC at the rate of £2.10 per week, by filing the form CWF1 with HMRC National Insurance Contribution Office.

Limited companies

- Within 9 months of the year end
  Pay over any corporation tax due.

- Within 10 months of the year end
  File (usually abbreviated) accounts with Companies House.

- Within 12 months of the year end
  File the company's corporation tax return with HMRC.

Chapter 7

New business – getting it, charging for it, getting paid for it

Creating YOUR new business policy

When the phone rings or the e-mail pings and you are asked to make a proposal, know what your game plan is. If you are really new to all this, you'll be dancing around the room and have already spent the mega-mounds of money you are about to make. Then reality strikes and you begin to think: what is the best way forward? Here are my rules.

New business rule 1: the first meet is free, after that we think about it

Once you know what you are up against, where do you go next? Always give a first meeting at no charge, and then keep that time sheet and build all the other pre-assignment meets into your budget (remember, YOUR budget that YOU see). If the business doesn't come after meeting three, it probably won't come at all.

New business rule 2: never give away the farm

Unless you know the people very well, never make a detailed proposal for the first meeting. I've done it, so has everyone else. In my case they took it, loved it and shut the door in my face. Months later I saw it being implemented by another consulting firm. Hard lesson learned. Now I give a broad outline and some likely costs to get the discussion moving. And I always leave some things out (and definitely any contacts or names of other people I would use). If anyone objects, the line, 'Well, I know you are busy, and I didn't want to bog you down in detail until we agree the basics' always works for me.

New business rule 3: if it looks to good to be true – it IS too good to be true!

Keep your feet planted firmly on ground. Consider the client. What do they look like, what do they represent? Check them out. Don't take anything at face value. Think, 'Do I really want to do business with these people?' Then phone a friend and ask the audience too!

New business rule 4: show me the money

In *any* new business venture, invoice one-third up front (plus that 10 to 15 per cent expense advance). If they are serious they will pay it. Don't commit until you get that. This will do two things: earn their respect, and also make sure you don't end up having to hire debt collectors. If they want what you have got to sell, they will pay.

New business rule 5: share your good news and get a contract

Pieces of paper (signed by both parties) *are* useful. Get a deal signed and sealed and file it with your lawyer. Again, if they really want you, this won't be a problem either.

Writing proposals that work

My somewhat cynical view is that few proposals ever get read in any great detail. Pressed-for-time executives probably read the opening creative bit and then turn to the costs. But there are – to my mind – several simple rules about getting proposals in front of prospects.

Writing proposals rule 1: make it original

Too often, I see proposals which have been tarted up from some standard example in a Microsoft Word file. While I may refer back to previous proposals, I always write them afresh. That way they seem to fit with a client's needs better. It takes time, but I personally believe (although I have no hard evidence for this) that it delivers a higher strike rate.

Writing proposals rule 2: make it short

As I said earlier, don't give away your secrets, but also keep it nice and short (you can send a longer specification-ridden version if you get the business) so that you get their attention.

Writing proposals rule 3: make it formal

Send an e-version by all means, but also send a proper hard-copy version. It looks professional and shows a certain amount of respect for the prospect and for the project you are bidding on.

Writing proposals rule 4: the 24-hour delay tactic

No matter how urgent, try and give yourself 24 hours to reflect on your proposal before you 'ship' it out. Close the office and come back the following day and reread it. I am certain you will change at least one significant item (usually that cheap budget line to try and keep initial costs down!).

Writing proposals rule 5: check it out!

So many proposals I see have really bad spelling errors and other faults. Make sure it not only looks good but is good. Get someone else to read it at least twice. Again, I guarantee you'll make corrections.

When to chase for the business

There should be a seminar on this subject. Reason? I have never met anyone who knows the real answer. Indeed, every time I meet with two of my good friends we discuss the psychology of when to call. Call too soon – you look eager. Call too late – you didn't want the business badly enough. Call on the wrong day – that's trouble too. My view has come down to this: when YOU think it is time to call, it probably is. I have agonised over this for so long that I am now considering just letting it run for 72 hours and following up, regardless of who it is or the type of assignment I am bidding on.

The trouble is that we begin to play mind-games with ourselves. We think that our prospective client is ignoring us. The reality is that there are a thousand-and-one other things on his or her desk that demand attention. Our big issue is a drop in the ocean to them. So we sit and fret or sulk and wonder. And what we wonder about is never anything to do with reality.

So my advice is send in your proposal and, after 72 hours, call. That gives you an acceptable gap not to look too eager, but just enough time to seem concerned that you get the business. Am I right? Frankly I haven't got a clue! On this one you are really on your own. But if you ever hear of a seminar on this that really works, let me know.

Schmoozing the PA

One way of upping your chances of getting in front of your prospective client is to schmooze the personal assistant. I spend a lot of time on that. Consequently, I rarely call my most senior contacts (they are never in their offices anyway). Just phone their PAs and have talks about how busy their boss is and stuff like that. Then you say, 'I'd like to get the chance of a meet' and you get on that list very quickly indeed.

> *Tip! The PA is your ticket to ride – use it and abuse it wisely.*

Setting fees, and other money worries

Setting a realistic fee level isn't easy for the first-timer. What you charge is determined so much by the business you are going to be conducting, the type of clients you will have and where you will be doing this. A young accountant starting out on his or her own in Cornwall is going to be charging very differently from a middle-aged, highly experienced accountant in London who wants to try their hand at going it alone. Similarly, a training consultant in the Midlands working mainly for the public sector is going to set fees differently to a personal coach for the director of a listed company in London.

My own view is that the very best way to begin to understand what to charge is ask. Yes, there's a lot of asking in this business! If you don't know anyone operating in your chosen independent profession, find someone. The easiest way to do this is embark on some market research. Pick up the local Yellow Pages, trade directories or local chamber of commerce handbooks (all available at your local library) and make up a list of likely targets. Then call them and ask about their fees, on the excuse that you want to consider hiring them. This is NOT a crime! Chances are you'll get some great ideas and also get an indication of what extras they charge and why.

Once you begin to understand the 'local' market, you can set your fees accordingly.

So, first know the market you are going to play in. By understanding it intimately, you can make a clear-cut decision about what you are going to do. If you are seeking volume, you

> *Tip! Remember, the 'local' market is the one you play in. If you are highly specialised, your local market can cover the globe. I know a guitar consultant who travels the world for rich clients. He has two 'competitors' that he knows of, but their fees are remarkably similar and one is in Japan and one in California. Your 'local' business is peculiar to you and those that also undertake it. Similarly, an independent specialised trainer will have 'local' competition, but only for people who require his services.*

might try undercutting the competition in your 'local' market. If you want to go for a high price, know why you are doing that. However, remember one thing – once you drop your price it isn't easy to put it up again.

Yes, we've all been there too. When business gets lousy, as it does from time to time, you will come under pressure to drop prices. Clients and prospects will tell you that your competitors have lowered prices by 25 per cent, or even more. This poses a test to your confidence, and also your business ability. Seldom are things as they seem. If you are going to stay in business, you may agree to take on some short-term assignments that keep your operations running. But never get into long-term commitments that way. Similarly, anyone who says that they have never cut their prices is definitely not telling the truth. What you need to do is limit the damage. Do it very much as a favour to your client, but make sure that they value and understand that decision. And get them back to the original fees as quickly as you can.

Sometimes, in really good economic times, prices do mushroom. Usually clients are happy to pay, because they are making good money too. So certainly there are times when fees do need a bit of correction. There is a kind of symbiotic relationship that develops. When the good times roll, you roll with them and learn to build up some fat for the bad days. When those bad days arrive, most clients want you to join them in the pain process. Looking fit and prosperous while your clients are on an extreme diet is not good.

Tip! Never, ever turn up at a client in a new car when times are bad – it is suicide.

The time-benders

Time is a peculiar thing – you can even stretch it to make money. Here's how to do it. Some years ago, I had a new competitor in town. Very aggressive and – it soon came clear – very much selling on price: a price seriously undercutting my own. After a few months, I was bidding on a piece of work and lost out. I asked – always ask, people can only say no – why we lost. 'Here's why', said my contact and she threw my rival's proposal (not really an ethical thing to do) across the desk at me. I looked at it. His hourly fees were almost half of mine. What they had done was buy on price. But they didn't really do that at all. They were mesmerised by the idea of a very low hourly fee (so was I!). There was no way anyone could make money like this. Then I looked at the rest of the document. Essentially, total fees for the project from my competitor and myself were the same. The only difference was that he was – when you examined the proposal closely – going to take a lot more time to do it.

Here's how it works.

If I bid £50/hour (using a six-hour chargeable day as a guide), that's £300/day.

If the project is estimated to take 5 days, that's £1,500.

If my competitor bids at £30/hour, that's £180.

But if he then takes twice as long to complete it, that's 10 days and £1,800.

Is that clever? No. That isn't the clever part. What you actually do (without telling the client, of course), is to complete the project in five days and bill them for 10.

The variable fee game

Unless you are purely in this independent existence for the money (in which case, go take a high-paid job somewhere instead), there are times when dropping your fees (although only YOU know that) makes really good sense. Assuming that a large part of your decision to go into business for yourself was prompted by the fact that you like what you do and have quite a passion for it, creating variable fee structures (for all sorts of reasons) makes a good deal of sense.

Indeed, variable fee structures are something that few other consultants (and certainly not the medium and large ones) can manage (usually because they have a lot of hungry junior consultants to feed and the system can't take this sort of thing); so once again it gives us real independents a true competitive edge.

My own version of variable fees is based on a lot of experience gained over the years. While I will charge a full rate for my services to anyone who is clearly able to pay, I'll come and go quite a lot for something that I really want to do because it will (a) do my own reputation a lot of good and (b) help with other projects I am involved in. Likewise, I will do pro bono work on the basis that, yes, of course, it helps others, but it also widens my network, adds to my own knowledge and so on.

Marking up work

If you use other independents to help you out, do you mark up their work when you bill the client? Frankly, I think it really is up to the individual and the circumstances. Over many years I have used other consultants, commercial artists, photographers, printers and so forth in my own assignments.

> *Tip! If you are using others to help you and their costs are going to be large (printing and market research come quickly to mind), get your suppliers to invoice your client direct. While you won't be able to put a mark-up into the system, you will do wonders for your cash flow.*

Where I have to really supervise a piece of work and co-ordinate the final parts, I mark up their work. If it is very straightforward, I don't. With large amounts, I also get my suppliers to invoice clients direct.

I believe that your suppliers (a key part of YOUR network, remember) need to be paid fast. If you pay them and then wait 120 days (about average for big company payments these days), you are going to be out of pocket and out of funds.

The mark-up game

Over the years, I have completed a large number of third-party assignments. These are usually fed to you by big consulting firms who either haven't the time or possibly the specialist expertise to fulfil them. It is always a useful insight into the world that we don't often tread, where fees reach heights most independents can only dream of. Most of my experiences have been bizarre.

I was asked – at 24 hours' notice – to write a speech for a senior executive. So paranoid was the agency about their client, that not only wasn't I allowed to meet them or get a briefing on the phone, I wasn't even to be told which company it was.

Some months later I played golf with a friend and his brother. We got talking after the game and he was recounting some humorous stories about his work and told one about this paranoid agency and this speech they had written for him. I quickly realised it was *my* speech. So (here we go with the asking again) I asked him if he could recall how much he paid. He told me. It was three times what I had charged. Guess who got the next assignment?!

Retainer business

In my part of consulting, retainers are but a distant memory. For those who have never come across them, it works like this. A company engages your services (usually for a fixed number of hours or days, plus any expenses incurred) on a long term (one- to two-year) agreement. For this you are paid a regular income, usually on the first of the month.

The trouble with retainers is that they are normally (and certainly for any around today) rather restrictive. First, they will usually stipulate who else you can work for. Second, they often end in a huge accumulation of unspent time, which you may find yourself having to work off long after the 'retainer' has expired, depending on the deal you so enthusiastically agreed.

My view, if I was offered a regular retainer today, would be to examine it microscopically from all sides, write my own version and get it witnessed by my legal adviser as well as the client.

Then again, if you can get an 'open' retainer that means if the client doesn't use your time in the course of that month (or time agreed) it is their loss, jump for it. If clients want to be silly with their money we are not in the business of discouraging them.

Expenses

You could write a complete book on expenses, possibly an encyclopaedia. But for the purposes of this book, it is important for any independent to understand that getting reimbursed (quickly) for costly outlays is vital.

I always ask (and always seem to get) an upfront advance on expenses (usually around 10 to 15 per cent of the fee estimate). This means that you are not turning yourself into a bank for your client, but are using a portion of their money to get a project operational.

Some consultants mark up expenses incurred by adding anything from 15 to 25 per cent to the total – I don't. When I make a proposal, I always make it clear that expenses are billed (and supported by invoices where required) as incurred and that's it. This must be a good policy. Since 1982, no one has ever refused to pay my expense invoices, and no one has ever asked for all those receipts. Frowned at a few, I imagine, but never refused to pay!

As a personal thing, I also like to pay for my own travel and then bill it to the client. Often, clients prefer to do it for you (usually because they get better deals than you do), and if you are just starting out don't worry, do it: they are paying and you're not. In the early days, anything that will provide sacrifices to the goddess of cash flow is very acceptable. More on travel is detailed on pp. 75ff.

Recovering development costs

Depending on the business you are getting into, business development costs (some call them market opportunity costs) can be quite considerable. Most consultants need to create programmes and concepts, and these take time and often real monetary expense to develop fully. My own view is that anything you do for yourself to enhance and grow the business is a real sunk cost. The way you get it back is to sell your idea. However, being asked by a client or prospect to develop some ideas is a different thing. What I always do is keep a strict record of the time (and the real expense) of such an exercise and build this into the final business proposal. Of course, not everyone works that way: but it does give you some way of recouping your costs and your time.

Again, much depends on what sort of business you are in. If you are in personnel training, you will have a need to create programmes and back-up materials (if only to convince a prospective customer of your professionalism). In this case these are true development costs that may never – in reality – be fully recovered. On the other hand, if a client asks you to develop something, charge them (time and expense).

Don't forget, as a consultant, clients will use you because they expect you to have the right ideas, the right programmes and the right information they require. This means that you have to have a development process (like that new business process) going on all the time.

Other costs include travel to prospect locations and those that crop up in doing early research on an idea. Planes, trains and motorcars, as well as hotels and other services needed to sustain us, cost money. Try and keep track of it all and assess how well you are doing. Ideally, when you finally make proposals, get as much of this up-front expense in there as you can, so that you can begin to reduce those development costs.

Of course, you may well find yourself involved in making a major (hugely time-consuming) proposal to a prospect and having it turned down flat. Console yourself and consider whether you can approach anyone else with this idea, or adapt it for other uses. Although virtually every proposal I make is a one-off event, there are always elements that can be re-used or re-developed in different ways. If you can get to be good at that, you can quickly reduce your overall development costs and the time involvement too.

Dealing with no-shows

Clients and prospects can be quite rude, you know. A colleague of mine runs personal development programmes and frequently has real difficulties because two or three from a group of ten not only don't show, but don't bother to call and say so. This is particularly galling when he is running free 'taster' seminars as part of his marketing effort.

To try and go some way to counter this, he came up with a great idea. When you register, you have to pledge to give £10 (€15), by giving your credit card details to a charity. If you don't show you 'donate' the £10. Not only does this shame people into calling to cancel, it has had the effect of actually reducing no-shows to a minimum.

Contracts and letters of engagement

Once someone on the client side has said 'Yes', it is time to get a piece of paper put together that clearly states the basic work to be done and the price to be paid for it. So many organisations have their own versions that it is pretty pointless suggesting your own. However, do try and get it set up right from the outset, as if something goes wrong this is your safety net. All too often (and I am as guilty as the rest) you get enthused and excited about a new assignment and go rushing off to get things started (often the reason for that is the ludicrous time-frame YOU have agreed to!): try and curb that urge. Get an e-mail or fax version, sign it and keep their version. Then get to work.

In these hectic days things happen fast. Takeovers, mergers, executive departures and organisational changes all bring havoc to independent activity. That contract or letter of engagement will ensure that you get paid if something goes wrong.

When the brief changes

In recent years, I can't recall a single consulting assignment where the original brief stayed the same throughout the duration of the project. This usually stems from the fact that most clients – but please don't tell them this – rarely have a clue about what they want and consequently give a really bad briefing.

Because of this, most independent consultants find themselves deep into a project when the brief changes and new elements get inserted into the programme. At this time, it is important that the agreement you have clearly states that changes are an additional cost that needs to be quoted for. Do this quickly. Call your client. Inform him of the changes that his firm requires and send him a revised budget and time-frame. The sooner this is done the better. Then when the new work is agreed have that added to the contract or agreement. What you don't want are any protracted negotiations, as these just detract from getting the real assignment completed.

However, I've never found it useful to bill every last red cent. If I am working on an assignment for, say, 15 days and I run over a day, I won't bill that extra time. I will however, make sure the client knows how generous I am. If I finish that 15-day assignment in 14 days I won't give him back any money either; so it is very much swings and roundabouts – some you win, some they win. Remember that it is always important to keep time sheets for each assignment so that, even if the client never wants to see them, you can assess the actual cost of the project. Very often in my business I am quoting 'blind', that is to say, putting together a quote for a client based on a request that I have never had before. Hopefully, I am experienced enough to get it about right, but the only way I know that I haven't screwed myself is to keep a daily track of how much time I have spent.

The gentle art of quoting

Just like selling, some independent consultants are naturally good at getting this right. Others are – and seem to remain – woefully inadequate. The key to getting the quote right is a complex formula that actually has very little to do with reality and a lot to do with perception – the client's perception. If they feel they are getting value for money that's all that counts. This is another reason for working with major firms, as they usually know how to buy consulting and they are expecting to pay for it.

As I said in an earlier chapter, I will never allow myself to get talked into anything where payment is dependent on results. It is your time you are selling and therefore that is what you are quoting. However, the formula is complex. When you are really eager to get a piece of business, you will be sorely tempted to reduce the number of days or squeeze down your hourly charges. In my experience this is not good and sets a bad precedent to yourself. I know that every time I have been worried about getting business in and I have reduced a budget another piece of business (at a much better rate of pay) has come in. What happens (and I tell my clients this too), is that you concentrate on the new piece of well-remunerated work and the other piece come a poor second. That old phrase that a labourer is worthy of his pay is very true. So when you quote think about reality. Decide what it is really going to take in terms of time to do the best job you can, and stick with it.

Evolving the client relationship

The smart consultant knows that once he is inside the corporate version of Troy, his secondary task must be to stay there. This isn't that hard. Presenteeism works better for consultants than anyone else. The fact that you are in front of XYZ's executives on a regular basis means that your chances of other assignments increase dramatically. Just because you are there, you will be given work, because it is a lot easier to give it to you than start the process all over again. So, the trick is to build confidence and reputation and volunteer a lot for assignments. In my experience, really busy managers are just relieved to get assignments off their desks and into some kind of action mode. If this may sound a little cyn-ical, it really isn't. Once a client gets to know you and your capabilities, they will feel comfortable and like having you around. Encourage this and develop strong relationships. I

> *Tip! In twenty-first century business, things can change very quickly. So don't put too many beans in that tin please. Keep as wide a range of clients and prospects as you can – you'll need them one day.*

know consultants who regularly take their clients to football, cricket and tennis events or have London theatre evenings. Very often hard-pressed exec-utives are grateful for these 'excursions', which underscore how much you value the relationship.

Getting paid

In my experience, most companies are pretty good at paying what they owe. There are exceptions, but you rapidly learn how to avoid doing business with those people. However, the most important thing about getting paid is up to you. It is simply getting your invoice in on time. Don't mess about. As soon as you can, get it in for approval. The main reason for this is that the modern corporation takes anything from 120 to 180 days to pay, so you want to give yourself the very best chance you can. Otherwise, cash flow can be seriously compromised.

> *Tip! Invoice as rapidly as you can, it will make at least 30 days difference in when you get paid.*

I have to say that in a career of over two decades I have only had two bad debts that I had to write off totally. In both cases the people went out of business, leaving huge debts, and there was nothing to be recov-ered. Luckily they were both for small amounts.

At other times, circumstances just catch up with you. A case in point was early in my solo career when I encountered what I would describe as the independent consultant's black hole. My client – a senior manager in a major multinational – was made redundant very suddenly. I had an agreement with him – including a working contract – but it had not yet been approved by his boss (the one who terminated him). I had done a great deal of work and had already billed for two-thirds of the assignment. I had never met my (now former) client's boss. The only thing to do was go and see him. I got a meet-ing arranged and flew to Paris and explained the situation in some detail. Maybe I was lucky, I don't know, but he had all that was owed paid that day. Personally, I believe that the act of going to see him made the difference.

Similarly, I read with horror a newspaper account of a corporate meltdown where I had a string on unpaid invoices. In the midst of a mass redundancy programme I again reached the managing director of one of the divisions and he personally took me to the accounts department and got my invoices paid in full. Personal relationships (and your client's PA) count big in these circumstances.

Creating embarrassment

Some years ago a relatively small firm owed me money. I knew they were in financial trouble and was concerned that they would eventually go out of business, leaving me with nothing after I had completed all the work. Phone calls, reminders and threats of legal action failed. So I had an idea. I had a cross-town courier service I used and one of their staff was the meanest person I had ever laid eyes on (he looked like a former boxer who had fallen on hard times). In reality he was a really nice person, but most people just looked at him and ran. What I did was to offer him 10 per cent of this outstanding invoice if he could collect. On his day off he turned up in the accounts department of this firm and asked for the money. They told him to wait. He did. Telling everyone else that came in that he was trying to collect the money and he wasn't going home without it. After two hours he emerged, a cheque for the full payment in hand. We deposited it in the bank within 10 minutes to make sure it didn't bounce!

A suitcase full of trouble

Sometimes independents really have to think outside the box to get the money they worked for. I had completed a major project for a London-based publisher. Although I had received my initial payment, two-thirds of the fees and the majority of the final expenses were still to be paid, and they had just been taken over by a rival after an acrimonious series of negotiations. My concern was getting paid in full. What I did was to arrive in London with a suitcase that contained all the manuscripts they required. I then sat in a café until their office boy appeared with a cheque. I took him and my suitcase to a bank where I had arranged to deposit the money. Once it was deposited I handed the office boy the suitcase. Extreme, but as it turned out probably necessary – six months later, the new owners went out of business. Further proving my point that working for large companies (or the public sector) is the best idea for a long-term career as an independent consultant.

What, I think, all this illustrates is that you need to really know your client and the risks that may be involved in working with them. Relationships and working styles vary hugely from place to place. A major multinational is very different from a consulting firm or the public sector.

Chances are that you will experience all of these and more. Understanding the differences is part of your guide to survival and ultimate success. While you may never work for or with all of them, there are very rewarding experiences to be had; and an assignment in one can be a huge learning experience, which can often transfer to another sector.

Working with different client groups

You are probably going to find yourself in a wide variety of work environments. I hope so. One of the most satisfying parts of an independent consultant's life (unless you really are a shy, retiring flower) is being able to experience different work places, patterns and probably politics too. I am now going to outline some thoughts on different employer groups, which may give you some ideas as you begin to widen your work horizons.

The big corporations

Most of my consulting work has been done for major multinationals. Depending on your expertise, this can be hugely rewarding both in job satisfaction and remuneration. Obviously it demands a great deal of flexibility, and usually travel away from home base for periods of time. For me this is more than compensated by the variety and scale of the work and the opportunities for ongoing learning and development that these sorts of assignments generate.

While it can be difficult to break in, the best way is often on the back of a bigger consulting firm that needs extra arms and legs on major assignments. When the bigger consulting firms get busy, they are often only too pleased to have third parties they can call on for help. It really is worthwhile going to see these people. It might take some effort to get on the radar screen initially, but it will be well worth the effort (see 'Never make cold calls – ever!' on pp. 100–101). Example: I have a colleague who has become a global traveller through lending his skills to due diligence efforts for acquisitive corporations. In these

> *Tip! Don't be discouraged just because it is a big multinational business. Often these places are a lot less sophisticated than you might think.*

cases he is hired and paid by the firm's consultants. Getting in at ground level for these types of assignments is not all that easy, but, if this is your sort of thing, the effort is well worth it.

Big corporations today don't have the army of internal support functions that they used to. Increasingly, areas like training and development, coaching, mentoring, market research, communications and so on are outsourced.

This kind of 'give it out to others' activity doesn't just take place at the head-quarters, but in divisions scattered around the globe. Getting the initial foot in the door might not be easy, but smart corporations are constantly on the look-out for specialists who can help them.

The big consultants

As I indicated above, the major consultants often use third-party help when the going gets busy. Indeed, I know several independents who work virtually exclusively for one or two big firms, using their unique talents to help meet client needs. Very often some type of specialist knowledge that you can sell, or experience of a particular industry or region, can get you hired.

Small and medium-sized enterprises

Depending on your skills and your career plans, any independent consultant can make a good living out of working for small and medium-sized enterprises. If you want to work within a particular geography, for example, it makes a great deal of sense to become established in a specific community. Certainly, getting business by word of mouth is more likely when working within a restricted geographic area. Joining local chambers of commerce and other trade-related groups also gets your face in front of the local business community. The only warning I would give is to make sure that you thoroughly check out the financial viability of prospective clients. Of course major multinationals go bust as well, but not with the same fatal consistency as smaller firms.

Public sector

Although I have little experience of the public sector, I do know consultants who have gleaned almost all their business from this area. Examples include two management consultants who have built up a lucrative practice advising local government on operational management issues, as well as a consultant in healthcare who has established herself firmly within the National Health Service. Again, it is all a question of getting in the first door. Often, assignments are given out to tender – especially in local government – and it is worthwhile checking out opportunities. A simple visit to your local council offices may unearth more than you expected. Additionally, local libraries and local newspapers usually advertise upcoming opportunities.

Non-government organisations

Non-government organisations (NGOs) are on the increase both nationally and internationally, and virtually all use consultants. While I know of many consultants who do this work because they are also in tune with the NGO's aims, they still can provide a solid income and a very rewarding career path. In many cases – in both national and international operations – the management of NGOs is excellent, and they like to work within very specific guidelines and with clear-cut and precise contracts. If this type of career appeals to you I suggest cups of cocoa and some late nights surfing the Web as the best way of getting to know what NGOs require in the way of external consultant support.

Transnational institutions

By this I mean everything from the European Union and the United Nations to the World Health Organisation and the World Bank. These types of institutions constantly spawn new initiatives and need help in carrying them out. Again, get access (use the Web) to their official publications, which explain a great deal about their current work and plans. I know several specialist independent consultants who seem to work exclusively for these types of institutions.

Maintaining and evolving client relationships

While we are going to look in-depth at developing the business in Chapter 8, it is worth saying a few words here about how to develop a long-term relationship with a client. First, what you have to get clear in your mind is whether this is a relationship based on the individual who feeds you work, or with the organisation that he or she works for. Ideally you can have both. Getting business these days can be hard work, so you want to get the most out of all your efforts. Therefore, I think that the most important aspect of evolving a business relationship is to try and spread yourself through a business and not be reliant on one person to give you work.

Part of the reason for this is straightforward. If your minder gets transferred, promoted or leaves, what happens then? If you are already known to others then you have a much better chance of surviving. That, of course, does not always happen. Too often in my experience your client leaves and is replaced with a new manager who brings not only his own ideas but his own external consultants with him. This is the nightmare scenario for all of us independents and one we can do little about. At that point, our only recourse is to follow our old client and hope that he has work in his new job.

Also, I think one of the biggest barriers to developing and enlarging a client relationship is our own failure to get across what we really do. All too often, when I analyse it (usually when it is too late!) I realise that I was hired in for a specific task, with the client using me for something they could not do easily themselves. Where I often failed (and possibly still do sometimes) is not to let my clients know about all the skills I have available. For example, if I get hired in to work on some employee communication strategy, they are not going to ask me to write the chairman's speech to the shareholders unless they know that's also what I do. It is this failure to advertise ourselves (when we have already sold ourselves) that probably loses an independent consultant more business than anything else.

Conflict of interest

I have had countless conversations with fellow consultants about what constitutes conflict of interest. My view is that I will only ever work exclusively for an organisation in an industry if it has me on a full retainer, long-term contract. Otherwise, work like a doctor and don't tell the other patients how ill you really are! Other views also prevail. Headhunters would be instantly swept out of business if they followed the 'you can only work for one client in each industry' rule that some firms try to impose. Where possible, I feel very comfortable (and usually ask to) signing a non-disclosure or confidentiality agreement with my clients. But today, it would be practically impossible to work for just one company in an industry, and we have to rely on our professional reputations as someone 'who keeps his counsel' to get us through.

The vanishing departments

Life for the independent consultant is not always easy. At times, however, it takes on a farcical tone too. Some years ago, I had – after long, protracted discussions – sold a large research project to a major consulting firm. One Thursday evening, I left their offices with a plan to come back on the Monday morning to finalise contracts and begin the work. When I got to the reception I asked for my contact. The receptionist looked a little surprised and then flustered. She made a few phone calls and finally a man appeared. By this time reception was filling up with visitors. My 'host' escorted me to a side office where he explained that my contact was no longer with the firm – he had been made redundant on the Friday after my Thursday meeting! When I asked after the others on the 'new' team I was working with, they had gone too. Indeed, a few quick calls on my mobile confirmed that the entire marketing department had 'vanished' overnight. They had been so traumatised by the whole experience no one had thought to call me.

And no, I never did get any more business from that firm. This story goes to show that it is NEVER in the bag until the day you have been paid.

Paying suppliers

I am scrupulous about paying people who work for me or provide goods and services. Reason? They are usually small too (or so big, like your phone company, that they will give you all kinds of hassle) and they need to be paid. Also, pay fast and you will be their friend forever, which is very useful when you need them in a hurry. Think about it. Who would you drop everything for, the client who pays you in 30 days or the one who pays in 120?

In any case, getting a reputation as a poor or late payer isn't good for your image (and word travels, believe me) and just isn't worth it. However, this is another reason to make sure that you have a good cash flow, so that all your suppliers get paid on time.

Agents and alliances

There will come a time when someone does you a big favour that results in a very nice piece of business. The question then is, 'How do I thank them?' Personally, I find it best to enter into some sort of formal or informal arrangement. On that sort of basis, a payment of between 10 and 20 per cent of the fees you receive is the most usual. This usually lasts for a period of 12 months.

Tip! The same obviously applies if you, as the consultant, are able to sell a project to another consultant. In this case, there are various ways to be remunerated, but I like to keep it simple and usually expect 10 per cent over the first year of any assignment (that is always of fees only).

In other cases, fees vary from 10 per cent in year one, to 7.5 per cent in year two and 5 per cent in year three. This of course makes it complicated, and I much prefer to pay a one-time flat fee per assignment. All my relationships like this are based on trust (which incidentally usually works both ways).

I have a series of these alliances, and our FutureWork Forum group (see p. 102) operates on the same basis. In that case, one of our members is the leader for that assignment and carries out all the invoicing and administration. Any other member of the Forum who gets involved gets paid for their time accordingly.

To give you some idea of what an agreement looks like, I have attached a sample version that I have used effectively for some years as Appendix 3.

Key learning points

- Set fees and stick to them, except under the direst of circumstances.
- As an independent, you can easily have variable fees to suit the type of work you are asked to do.
- Give prospective clients one free meeting, then decide how you play it. Try and charge for your time from meeting two.
- Never give away all your ideas in a proposal. Keep something back to give you security.
- Remember! If it looks to good to be true – IT IS!
- Get a contract – especially for new business.
- When making proposals: make it original; make it short; make it formal; wait 24 hours to check it out; AND CHECK THE SPELLING.
- Make the PA your pal, he or she is the link to the client.
- Never, ever, agree to being paid by results. Your time is precious, get rewarded for using it.
- Unless you are on a retainer, conflict of interest should not arise. If it does, weigh your options: just how much do you want to be locked in?
- Always pay small suppliers as quickly as you can. A reputation as a good payer is the right one to have.
- Agents and other 'business-getters' will expect a minimum of 10 per cent of any business they bring you. Remember this should apply to fees only.

Chapter 8

Developing the business

Appearances count. Get a sun lamp, maintain an elegant address even if you live in the attic; patronise posh watering holes even if you have to nurse your drink. Never niggle when you're short of cash.

Aristotle Onassis

I keep six honest serving men
They taught me all I knew
Their names are What and Why and When
And How and Where and Who.

Rudyard Kipling

So, you've made it! You have created a stable, sustainable business. You have clients who appreciate your skills and counsel. You have a network that you resolutely maintain. You have some cash in the bank and things are not looking too bad at all. So what happens next?

The answer to that depends entirely on who you are and what you want to achieve in the future. For example, if you are content to stay as a solo operator and be a healthy, yet small, fish in a small pond, that's fine. Well it is fine until the day you change your mind, at least.

On the other hand, if you want to do new things and take the business in new directions and search for new consulting worlds to conquer, you are going to have to think long and hard about how to do it.

However, in my experience, you rarely have that clean-cut choice of whether to stick with what you know or change for something different or new. Quite simply, your business changes. Every day something is not quite the same as the day before. Just like a giant corporation, your little independent consulting firm is under pressure. And pressure bends things into new shapes. If we don't evolve, we will find ourselves with a business that doesn't meet the needs of our clientele; certainly not the way it used to. And that is easy to understand. All we need to consider is the impact of one thing – technology – on our business to realise that over the years that pressure has pushed and pulled us in all sorts of new directions.

Furthermore, our clients will demand new ideas, new solutions, new methods of working. If we are to remain successful we have to be able to meet and – hopefully – exceed those demands and expectations.

All of us – on a day-to-day, week-to-week basis – have to be aware of the evolving needs of the marketplace we operate in, and what that means to how we respond. Therefore we need to make choices about which direction we go next, what investments we need to make and what new skills we will need to acquire. You can be sure of one thing: sometime in the next 24 months, demand for part of what you offer the business community will slow (or disappear forever). So what are you going to replace that with?

It could be a simple change in the law that offers tax credits for learning on a huge scale that prompts the rise of a host of new competitors, or an emerging technology that threatens to automate one of your processes and remove your competitive edge; whatever it is, you need to be ready to change to meet that sort of challenge. And in talking to independent consultants with all sorts of skill sets and talents, it quickly becomes clear that everyone is vulnerable and that our existence (and our long-term success) depends on surviving in a world of constant, ever more rapid change.

Sure, we all know people who have been doing the same thing for the past 10 years. But I bet none of us know anyone who has been doing the same thing – and dispensing the same advice – for 20 years. And for how long can decade-old advice be relevant anyway?

The business, YOUR business, needs to move; forward might seem the most sensible option.

You can move forward in several ways:

• stay as a solo operator, but stay aware of the market's shifting sands
• form an alliance, joint-venture or partnership with others
• hire in people (there are pitfalls to doing that)
• contract out (there are pitfalls to doing that)
• consciously shrink the business.

Let's look at these in more detail (there are guides to the legal issues on pp. 108–109).

The solo operator

I know many solo operator consultancies where the person is only too pleased to remain that way. Sure, they may ask for outside help on an ad hoc basis, but essentially they remain true independents. There is nothing at all wrong with this. Many of those I know make a good living doing work that they really like (often they are highly specialised, even within a narrow niche of expertise). The only advice that I would give them is to make sure they stay up-to-date with their own special area. Interestingly, this is something most of them do by habit, as in many cases they make most of their income from working for other consultants who don't want to develop their expertise in-house. Sudden change is unlikely to concern them, as they seem to evolve along with the businesses they consult to.

Alliances, joint-ventures and partnerships

Too many independents have made the fatal mistake of hooking up with others and finding that they have lost the 'soul' of their own business in the process. If it is possible, my advice is to begin with a loose alliance (so no legal commitments and no shares swaps). If that works, then consider just how compatible you will be.

I continue in several *alliances* with other consultants whom I respect and feel comfortable working with. But, after my own bitter experience of a partnership, I will keep it just that – an oral agreement, with both understanding that. There is no reason that this sort of loose alliance cannot last for many years without requiring any kind of formality. For the independent consultant who values just that – independence – it is probably all that is required. The huge upside is that you can make your own decisions on who you work with, who you work for and in just what direction you want the business to go.

Joint-ventures and *partnerships* demand a lot more in terms of commitment, as well as throwing up lots of legal issues. My view is that you need a great deal of good advice before you plunge into one of these. Taking a lot of time to really understand the motives of the other parties for the making the deal pays off.

Recently, I witnessed a two-man independent firm sensibly, in my view, backing off from an alliance with a US consulting group. All was well in the early wooing stages. Then it became increasingly clear that their cosy world (where they made their own decisions and set their own work times) would be deeply affected by any formal relationship. Their first inkling of trouble was when they discovered that they were spending a huge amount of time in transatlantic conference calls setting sales and business development targets. As one of them told me, 'In all these hours talking about doing business, we could have been doing it, instead of just talking about it.'

This move to be within part of a more formal structure can easily be a setback to those of us who are true independents at heart. Certainly, there is an increase in the time spent on 'staff' meetings, reports, memos, budgeting and the like – all time that takes away from the process of meeting client needs.

Hiring staff

The easy answer to this is, 'JUST SAY NO!', but that is hardly a practical piece of advice. However, unless you know that you have long-term work assignments that are signed, sealed and set in stone, think carefully about a move of this kind. As every independent knows, hiring staff falls under the same category as buying a boat: there are two great moments, the day you buy it and the day you sell it. With staff it is easy to hire, not always so easy to fire. Legal aspects of employment (not the least social security costs) make the exercise an increasingly tough proposition for the small firm.

Consider carefully what this new member of your business is going to do. Could a contract worker do it as well? Will he or she be fully occupied? Will he or she be capable of developing?

On good days it gives you a nice feeling to see your team toiling away. On others it produces dark clouds of concern. If you cannot guarantee that you can fully occupy them five days a week, think of another solution. Also, when you hire them, ask yourself the question, 'Will they be able to help develop the business?' For the small consulting firm this is a vital attribute. Indeed, unless you are just adding some type of personal assistant, any other hires need to begin to bring in business and pay for themselves (or at least part of their upkeep). In doing that, they can often play to their strengths and open up new lines of opportunity.

> *Tip! When you hire, try and take on someone who, while being in tune with how you do business, also has some attributes or skills you don't have. This really can help 'round out' a small firm.*

Contracting out

If you cannot justify the outright hiring of employees, then it is far better to develop some long-term links with those who can help you. The advantages to this are pretty clear. The most important one is that it gives you flexibility.

You can hire people on short-term agreements and then wait until another assignment comes in before using them again. If you analyse this type of contract activity over a year or more, you should see that it is a lot more cost-effective than having people on the payroll who you have to remunerate whether they are doing client work or not.

Certainly, in this increasingly outsourced age, using contract workers is a growing trend. As I pointed out earlier, many specialised consultants make their living on contracts from other businesses (it may well be how you make much of your own income).

So flexibility and cost are the two main advantages, and often these contractual deals can develop into long-term working relationships. However, as with everything else, there are some disadvantages as well.

The two to be most concerned about are loyalty and availability.

While you cannot expect anything like 100 per cent loyalty from anyone you use as a contractor, you need to be careful (especially in the early days of a relationship) just how much information you share. Time and again over my career, I have heard the sad news that yet another independent colleague has been 'done over' by one of his contracted helpers. This is usually through letting them get too close to the client and them then taking over the work (often at promised – but rarely ever realised – savings). It is a hard, cruel world out there, and some people will do almost anything to secure business.

The other issue is availability. Possibly the only real advantage of having people on your payroll is that they are there to work for you alone (it is, of course, your job to keep them gainfully employed!) and so the issue of availability doesn't really arise. However, working with outsourced workers means that you cannot always guarantee that they will have the time when you need it.

Tip! Keep your 'casual' contractors at arm's length from your clients until your relationship is well established and fully understood.

My solution to that has always been to find several people that I really like to work with and then give them enough business to 'buy' their loyalty and their availability. You will quickly know what that is for different people. But don't forget that if you don't use someone for months on end, you will probably have to do that trust-building exercise all over again.

Personally, I would much rather work with a squad of carefully chosen 'contract' workers (so I can get the best niche consultant for whatever I need) than hire people (and try to make them do everything). This certainly isn't everyone's view and I am sure it depends on your style and your long-term objectives for the business.

Consciously shrinking the business

Ask many successful consultants to name the time they were happiest (not richest or most successful, but happiest) and most will tell you it was when they started out. Life, in retrospect at least, seemed simpler and more focused. It is not surprising, then, that many consultants who have built up highly successful practices often consider the idea of going back to the solo life again. There are a large number of reasons for this, but often it is that quest for a better quality of life or, as I mentioned earlier in the book, a chance to pursue other interests. I took the decision to shrink my own business some years ago. Starting out on my own and building up to a group of around 15 people was fun. But I have to say that those early years trying to make it on my own were perhaps the best. Now I work alone again, carrying out assignments that interest me and give me opportunities to meet and be involved with interesting organisations and individuals. In that, I consider myself lucky. I have been able to go, in a career of 30-plus years, from corporate life, to independent consultant, to business owner, and back to a solo operator. Hopefully, I am wiser now. Also my network has grown and, as I have been stressing throughout this book, has been assiduously maintained and added to.

There is never a right time to become – or return to the life of – a solo consultant. It is all a question of what is right for you. What it takes is to stay as honest with yourself as you can be.

Checking out the marketplace

Whichever way you decide to go to develop the business, you must keep up-to-date. Membership – and possibly an active interest – in professional associations can go a long way to help; if nothing else, it offers the opportunity to 'steal' ideas from your colleagues! The market does move: new ideas, trends and opportunities come and shake up our established view of our chosen professional area. So knowing what is going on is vital.

Equally, being aware of world events and putting those into a context that applies to your business can help you to see emerging trends before they impact you too greatly. I also believe that clients appreciate a consultant who seems to know what is going on in the big world and can relate it easily to their business: it just makes them feel that little bit more comfortable with employing you.

What that means is investing in information delivery. While the World Wide Web can be a source of a lot of material, I still think that the hard-copy written word makes you really read. It is also very useful for tearing out and taking with you on trips. I do a lot of my catch-up time on trains and planes.

What you choose to read depends a great deal on your own business activity. But if you are involved in any way with consulting outside your own country, then you may find it useful to look at my own reading list.

- Each morning and evening (and more frequently if I am working from my home workspace) I use the BBC News website – just to be aware of what is happening. www.bbc.co.uk/news
- Every morning (as I have for the past 30 years) I read the *International Herald Tribune*, because it is the quickest way to get world coverage of issues.
- Similarly, I read (or rather scan) the *Financial Times*.
- Every week I get *Business Week*, and more recently I have been taking the UK publication *The Week*.
- Other subscriptions that add to my professional view of the world include *Fortune*, *Harvard Business Review* and the *New York Review of Books*.

All these keep me up-to-date in the more general areas of world affairs but also report in-depth on areas that I am most active in and need to know about. In addition, I read a lot of junk stuff too (and also watch MTV and other specialist TV channels) to stay in touch with emerging trends and understand better the emerging world of work. I am a sort of magazine junky and will read anything and everything. I find that all of it helps me in my day-to-day work, because it provides ideas, contacts, and lines on new trends that keep you AHEAD of your clients, which is where you want to be.

Personally, I find that there is no substitute to being well-informed and no excuse for being poorly informed about areas that may affect your clients. It can certainly be the 'decider' between you or someone else getting an assignment. The other issue is that if you want to make presentations or write articles to impress your peers and prospects, it is much more readable if you are able to put your stuff into a world context. If you don't know what's going on you can't do that.

Keeping up to speed

Just as the media plays an important role in keeping you up to speed on world and industry affairs that affect your clients, so personal development helps you to be a much more useful consultant.

By that I mean that you don't just have to give advice and counsel, you need to go back to school occasionally and take some instruction too.

Seminars, workshops, conferences and debates are all important for keeping you aware of what your profession is up to.

Likewise, personal development programmes help to focus on areas of self-improvement. Rather like getting a health check, my view is that it is a good idea to sign yourself up for some type of personal development programme (if only because it will get you out of the professional rut for a few days).

Indeed, many independent consultants I know say that they don't go to professional conferences or even development seminars for the content, but just as an opportunity to reflect on where they are going and what they really want to do. Down-time, even for the most eager solo operator, is a good thing.

Marketing others

If you have found yourself hiring staff, you are going to have to make some quick choices about whether or not you want to sell their services. While this depends to a great extent on what their role is, if they have any kind of contact with the client you need to make sure that they are an asset to the business rather than a turn-off. You know what is expected by the client: your new hire (or even your contracted helper) doesn't. This can make for difficult relationships as you try and make sure that this new person not only fits in with your way of working, but also is respected and appreciated by your clients. Over the years, I have had all sorts of problems with this (everything from poor – to completely inappropriate – dress sense, to basic attitude), and it is never easy to resolve.

However, my advice would be to develop your new hire's contact with clients on a slow, but steady learning curve, hopefully ironing out any bumps along the way. Just don't forget the very basic rule: this is your business and your clients. Manage them both the way you see is best. Don't compromise. If a new hire – or new contractor – can't work the way you do, remove them. In the longer term you'll have to anyway. It will just cause a lot more trouble to delay.

> *Tip! Never forget that with a small consultancy the client is buying YOU. If you add personnel he is still buying YOU. How you manage your people is your problem. Do it badly and it will reflect on you.*

Keeping your culture

In may sound a little grandiose to talk about culture in a one- or two-man outfit – but it's not so. You HAVE created your own culture, from the moment you made that decision to strike out on your own. Therefore, it is really important that as soon as you start to add other people to your firm they truly understand what your consulting services stand for. If they don't 'get it' you won't be able to properly retain that cultural 'feel' that you have taken – possibly – years to create and that your client appreciates so much. So, keep the culture intact. Make it clear from day one (write them down if necessary) that these are your cultural mores and the way you do business. Make sure your new associates or employees really sign up to this.

Have you lost focus?

While many independents have built up strikingly successful 'boutique' consulting firms from very modest beginnings and are able to thrive and prosper, others come to realise that this often takes them away from their reasons for starting up in the first place.

I know of many independents who created a business, only to find that they had removed themselves from the day-to-day, hands-on part of the operation.

'It just stopped being fun,' one told me. 'After 10 years of growing the business, I realised all I was doing was working like hell to bring in business to feed the people I had hired.'

Another, who created an award-winning design consulting firm, told me, 'One day I realised that in the past six months all I had done with a pen in my hand was to sign expenses for my employees!'

In both these cases, the consultants went back to their roots and their real reasons for starting up: being involved in the day-to-day action and solving challenging problems. Interestingly, it seems the more people I meet the more are determined that situation either won't happen to them, or that when it does they'll know what to do about it. Keeping a sense of focus and knowing what you are in this business to do is important, and you should never lose sight of that. As another, recently returned to single status consultant explained, 'I just wasn't happy. I had everything I thought I should have. Then I realised the buzz had gone. The reason, when I sat down and thought about it, was that I wasn't made for managing others. I was made for getting things done – my way.'

Tip! Make it an annual event. Take a day off and sit and think about where you are today, where you've come from and where you REALLY want to go. What's going to make you happy? Do you need to make changes? If so, how long will you give yourself to achieve them?

Recently, on a plane to Inverness in Scotland my fellow passenger turned out to be an independent consulting veterinary surgeon. He had built up a highly successful inner-city practice, until one day he realised this was not what he wanted. He knew enough people (that network again!) to get a flow of work, mainly from government departments. He now lives and works from his house bordering a Scottish lochside, but travels the world researching and lecturing for his Westminster clients.

Changing pricing structures

Several times a year I meet recently independent consultants who tell me that business is good – better than they ever dared hope – but they are working all hours of the day and night to meet the demands of their clients. To their question, 'What should I do, Mike?' I have a quick, trite response: 'Put up your fees.'

There's a theory held by some of us, and proved by many of us (see box), that fees are what you want to make them. Slavishly monitoring the market and then following the average price is no more scientific to my mind than sticking a pin in a column of figures. Basically, people who want YOU will pay you what they think you are worth.

True, in economic downturns there will be pressure on prices, but that should not mean that you are reluctant to return to a good stiff (yet honest) hourly or daily rate as soon as you can. Even if you have been screwed down or held back by current clients, you should always begin anew with those you are signing on for the first time.

This is one of the great 'secrets' of the independent consultant. You aren't bound by stringent fee structures, like many larger firms are. If you work for a medium or large-sized firm, you can't easily return to your boss and say, 'Well I couldn't get our day rate, but they did agree to one that is 25 per cent less.' Your boss – whose annual bonus is normally calculated on fee turnover – will not be best pleased to say the least.

The 50 per cent solution

Note that this only works in good economic times. If you are really busy and working all hours, put up your prices by 50 per cent on the next quote you give your client. There is a good chance they won't even notice if they too are very busy.

My colleagues and I have tried this over the years and it ALWAYS works in terms of total bottom line, because even if you lose 25 per cent of your business you work less, but still make the same overall fee income. WARNING!: As I said, don't try this in a recession. Not even when your client is mad about you!

However, as individual consultants – or even small boutique firms – we can (and usually do) operate on a sliding scale of prices. As I have already outlined, this allows you to take on interesting work that may not pay the best, but can lead to other opportunities. But it also allows you to work in different categories of business.

Tip! Never publish your fees. Keep them flexible, it opens up opportunities. Big firms expect to pay top dollar (in my experience they don't do 'cheap'. YES, you can quote too low, believe me). On the other hand, small firms expect a decent rate, but often this leads to extended business.

For example (and I hope I don't live to regret this), if I am working for a major multinational corporation I will charge a higher fee (or rather my usual fee) for any work I do. However, there are other small firms, where I am interested in the work but know I will never get it at my 'usual' full-fee rate. So, I compromise and usually everyone's happy.

Working with the competition

These days, I am not too sure what a competitor really is, so I am very open to working with just about anyone as long as they have a decent reputation and it is going to be an interesting project. In fact, this can be a good way of boosting your business. All of us get busy at certain times, and none of us want to turn work away (it never comes back). Therefore, if you can get a working agreement with one or more of your competitors to help them out when they have a rush on (and the same in reverse), I see nothing wrong in doing this. Where issues of confidentiality come into the equation or it is a particularly sensitive assignment, I would always clear it with the client. But if it is basic boiler-plate work, and as long as you have control over the final output, it can be a useful and practical solution.

Nightmare strategies

I think every independent consultant – even the very, very best – has had their equivalent of Black Monday. That dreaded day when the bottom falls out of the market and all your clients go into an emergency crash-dive, sealing off the entrances and communicating with no one. I've been there, and so have all my friends and colleagues in the business. If you meet a consultant who tells you that he has come through every recession without it having any effect, DON'T do business with him!

So what do you do? Well, I think that this sort of thing is as much about psychology as anything else. Here are a few thoughts:

- Never EVER tell anyone outside of your immediate confidantes that business has just tanked. That is an imperative.
- Go on with business as usual. Step up your business development time and investment. Your job now is to attract more business. But don't change your attitude: just increase your exposure to clients.
- As long as you believe in what you are doing, be prepared to throw money into the business – isn't that what that six months' survival money (that I talked about in Chapter 1: see p. 4) is there for?
- Stay, and look, confident. Although it may seem you are all alone, believe me, it has happened to everyone.
- Remember that shoulder to cry on. Use it. Phone a friend.
- Don't drop your prices or write crazy 'anything-to-get-the business' proposals, you will quickly regret it
- Launch an initiative that will get you noticed: run a seminar, a survey, an on-line newsletter (all excuses to contact and talk with your network). Don't hard sell: offer help and advice, it will be appreciated. They may know or suspect you have a few problems, but they will respect you.

And if it stays bad?

- Examine your outgoings. Is there anything you can cut that will save the bottom line? Sadly, if you are working from home there won't be much. However, with your costs on the floor, any new business coming in flows quickly to the bottom line without getting sucked away by expenses.
- Chase any outstanding debt and push for payment to keep cash flow.
- Go and see your bank manager and check out the options you might have.
- Finally: really PUSH your network HARD. Yes, do it. Hopefully you'll only have to do this once in every 10 years! Go and ask for work. It might be slightly demeaning, but it's a whole lot better than no business at all or, the even worse alternative, getting a REAL job!
- Look on the bright side. Hard as it might be, if you have survived as an independent consultant for any length of time, while it might take you three to six months to drum up significant new business, it will come. That can only happen if you really believe in yourself and what you offer. Self-doubts about whether you are really any good only generate negative energy.

The day the world fell in

I've been to the edge of the abyss. In the last 20-plus years there have been three recessions. I survived the first two very well. Recession three was unusual in that it hit every part of the world and most industries went down together. In my case my three biggest billing clients put up the shutters within a month of each other. That tends to concentrate the mind somewhat! Luckily, I had a good cash situation and was able to ride out the storm while seeking new business. It is never easy: it takes a lot of hard work and an ability to face rejection. Sometimes when you see those people with jobs, you feel a little jealous. Until the next time you call up and find that they have been ejected as 'superfluous to requirements'. That's when you realise that the flexibility the independent consultant has is the key to their survival. Certainly I wouldn't want to be anything else.

Bail-out strategies

Of course consultants, like others, do get tired and old. Many of them dream of selling out to someone else and enjoying a well-earned retirement. In my view independent consultants at this stage of life fall into two distinct categories:

- those who want to hang up their keyboards and PowerPoint clickers
- those who want to just keep on going, doing 'a little of this, and a little of that'.

For many of those in the first category, the idea of passing on the business to someone else is a possibility. Trouble is that if the business is just YOU, there isn't much to sell. After all, you can hardly leave your brain behind when you close the door for the last time (at least not yet anyway). In observing individuals and small groups trying to cash in on what they have created, I regret to say that most of them have been doomed to disappointment. In most cases any deal is subject to complex earn-out agreement rules whereby the seller has to stick around two, three, four or five years, and final compensation is based on the value of the business at that time. And, as I commented above, many individuals will be upset to see how little what is, after all, their life's work is valued.

True, there are always exceptions. Yet even these don't seem entirely satisfactory. The last one that I knew of that worked had the founder pounding the pavements for his soon-to-be American masters, pushing new business as hard as he could (something he had never had to do or that had even occurred to him before). The whole transaction left a bad taste and lost him a lot of respect and credibility in the marketplace.

Frankly, the ones who seem happiest are the good friends that I still work with who have reached their sixties and are still putting in the hours. Not as many as they used to by any means, but still keeping very active and very sharp. A lot of these people have forgotten more than a newly minted Indie knows, so they are very valuable. They are the elder statesmen of their profession, called on to provide words of wisdom, still get things done and talk a lot at conferences. They still make an income, but they have usually reached that age where money ceases to be the major concern. However, they have the time for long lunches with their friends (just like independent consultants did in the heady 1970s and 1980s) and open access to a lot of the great and good. They are useful, often quietly powerful and with networks to die for. Hope I end up like that!

A final thought

However you decide to develop your business (and only you can do that), I really do think that you have got to try and do this within the context of keeping that passion and work culture that you started out with. Get too corporate (too organised, too bureaucratic?) and you can lose so much of what made you become a consultant in the first place. Independent consultants – whatever their specialisation – are a unique breed of people. Most of them are self-motivated and, importantly, self-regulated. They know HOW and WHY things happen. They know what it takes to make and sustain success. So before you make major changes, please carefully consider what you want to get out of it and what it will do to the business you began. Then, when you have answered that, give yourself a time-frame to make your new plans work. And have a get-out strategy as well. Sooner or later, the real independent consultant will reassert himself or herself. As I said at the beginning of this book, we are not entrepreneurs. We are consultants who provide very special and much-needed services to the public and private sector. Every day our numbers are growing and will continue to do so. Whatever your plans, wherever you go, the drive and the dream that got you started needs to be part of your professional business offering.

Key learning points

- You don't NEED to move your business forward. Listen to your own voice – what do you really want?
- If you want to create an alliance or a partnership, try it out for some time before you commit to any legal structure.

- Hiring staff is a huge investment. If there are other ways, try those first.
- Contracting out business works for flexibility, but loyalty and guaranteed availability are not easy to find.
- There's nothing wrong with shrinking the business if you want to develop new interests.
- You need to stay always up-to-date. Clients expect advice and counsel based on a real awareness of the current climate.
- If you do hire in staff, remember it is YOUR business. Hang on tight to that culture you have created.
- Check out that in all your success you haven't lost focus on why you began the business.
- And when (or if) it all goes wrong, tell a few close confidantes and that's all. Never tell the whole world you're in trouble – go on with business as usual.

Chapter 9

What's next for the independent consultant?

> Never work before breakfast. If you have to work before breakfast, eat your breakfast first.
>
> *Josh Billings*

Making predictions can be hazardous at the best of times. Trying to peer into the future of independent consulting is not easy. For most of us who have been around for years, we have seen the whole business change more than once. So the easy way out is to fall back on what I said in the last chapter: you have to accept that change takes place all the time and you have to adapt your business proposition to match that.

Unfortunately, that isn't giving you much to go on. So here is a highly personalised view of what's coming over the next five years. Just don't hold me to it!

More competitors AND more opportunity

I have little doubt that we are going to see an ever more crowded market as more and more people take up the challenges of working for themselves. Everywhere I look it seems that there are vast numbers of new entrants to the marketplace, all eager to prove that they have the skills to make it on their own.

Quite frankly, I don't see this as a bad thing. The main reason for this is that there is an increasing amount of business too. From my viewpoint, many mainstream businesses in both the public and private sector are reluctant to return to high levels of full-time staff. Most of them, it seems, would rather outsource specialised work to external suppliers. Equally, as more and more work becomes intensely specialised, companies feel that they get a better deal hiring talent when they need it for short-term assignments rather than keeping it on the books.

This is borne out by the massive increase in the temporary, or interim, workforce in both Europe and the USA; a trend that shows no signs of slowing down. For years, employment experts have predicted real changes in how people get jobs, and this looks like finally coming to fruition. This opens many new doors of opportunity for the independent consultant, which we are only just beginning to see.

In the course of putting this book together I have spoken to scores of independent consultants who have basically outsourced themselves from their former workplaces and taken a tiny piece of the business with them. In some cases examples border on the farcical.

For example, a publisher I know was fired after 15 years in a job because she was the longest serving employee, and therefore (corporate logic decreed) the most expensive. Having terminated her – with full redundancy payments, I hasten to add – they then turned around and asked her if she could 'Please, please, please' act as the editorial consultant on the two publications she used to work on as they had no one with the expertise to do them. It gets worse. She called me and together we worked out the time it would take her, and the rate she should charge per day. Last year she made 150 per cent of her previous annual salary from the comfort of her own home. They are signing her up again.

Stories like this abound and are going to increase. When you talk to big corporations these days, you quickly realise that they don't actually like people very much. They are messy and prone to breakdown. So, if you can banish them from your offices (saving on office space too), and still get them to do the work, so much the better.

We are all seeing the reality of the 'virtual' office. And that is the playground of the independent consultant. Whether you are editing books, coaching people, handling legal claims, doing the books or creating sales campaigns, more and more companies would rather have you at a distance than on their premises. The great thing is that this is a truly win-win situation. You can get paid well (certainly as well as you were when employed), and they can save money by not having to worry about social security, pensions, healthcare and those pesky office costs.

Technology takes over

Whether we like it or not, technology will drive how, where, why and when you work, and possibly what you work at too. For most independent consultants – especially those working from their homes – technology-related costs will be the single most expensive budget item (and you will need to be smart and budget upgrades and the like into your operating plan).

Breakthrough technologies allied to breakthrough applications of those same technologies will govern a lot of what the independent consultant does next. We can already work fairly efficiently at a distance; tomorrow those distances will be even greater. Why sit 50 miles from your client in some rainy, grey suburb in northern Europe, when you can do your work from a sun-kissed veranda overlooking the Mediterranean? I already know people who do this, flying in to see their clients once a month or so.

This, I consider, will be the next big trend for many of us. Apart from the odd desk-bound manager who gets insanely jealous (and, yes, there are some like that!), most intelligent corporate types look to the quality of the work rather than where you do it from. But before you haul out the bucket, spade and beach towel, a word of caution. If you do decide to move, please pick a place where you can get back to your clients quickly and reliably. Quality of work counts, but so does availability.

Here's a cautionary tale. I once knew an IT consultant who bailed out and went to live in the Outer Hebrides. His work arrived on-line. For a year he was happy, going back to see his former work colleagues every three months. It looked idyllic. It looked too good to be true. And, as I have said throughout this book, if a thing looks too good to be true it probably is.

A year after he started work, I interviewed him for an article I was writing. I asked him, 'Apart from the local way of life, what is the best thing about working at a distance from your company?' Without hesitation, he replied, 'Office politics.'

Six months later, my interviewee had lost his job. Reason? Office politics. Basically, he hadn't been around to defend his position when the first round of job cuts came along. His work 'colleagues', probably mildly jealous anyway, had seen to it that he was the first to go.

The lesson here is that, yes, technology can free us, but it needs to be managed. Sadly, unless you are a one-of-a-kind genius, being away from the action makes you vulnerable. That isn't technology, that's human nature.

All the same, the ability of virtually all of us to invest in what is now relatively cheap technology does make setting up on our own a workable proposition. These days £1,000 (€1,500) will get us access to the same kind of technology our corporate brethren have access to. But *how* you use it will continue to drive the role of the independent.

As I have already said in previous chapters, new breakthroughs like multi-location video conferencing will change forever how we meet. Some consultants will develop this as a core skill, giving them huge advantages over those who don't do well 'on camera'.

And this is the other thing. We will need to stay up-to-date all the time. That old-fashioned idea that we learn (how to be an accountant or a psychologist, for example) and then spend the next 30 odd years practising is SO obsolete. Everyone who expects to survive as an independent will have to keep on learning. And as those technologies arrive we will have to learn not only how to use them but how *best* to use them, for ourselves and to improve our offering to our customers.

All of us are so much more productive today than even five years ago. We don't need much back-up support. We can turn out reports and proposals in hours rather than days. We can book our own travel, order our supplies on-line. Everything, it seems, can be achieved from our own desks. Except one thing: getting that face-to-face time with the client.

Shorter relationships

At the risk of sounding pessimistic, I think that we are entering an age where long-term consultant–client relationships will practically cease to exist. Of course there will always be the exceptions (the independent financial consultant who does a local client's annual return for 20 years), but for most of us, our relationships will be short and intensive. And we had better be able to adapt our workstyle to this emerging model.

I believe that we are headed into a period of major disruption. Following years of recession, we are now seeing an upsurge. This may auger well for the independent consultant in terms of more work being around, but it also means that those who give us the work are going to be a lot more unstable. Truth is that inside public and private organisations there is an increasing 'churn' of executives as they begin to switch jobs. This is happening both internally (being moved to another position) and externally (finding a new job in a new firm).

Added to this are two other indicators:

- Executives are increasingly busy, and have less and less time.
- Merger and acquisition activity is on the rise.

What all this does is create an interesting dilemma for the independent consultant, because it is harder to organise that face time with your clients as they have little time for outside 'interference', and you may well find a new incumbent in that manager's chair.

So our networks will need to expand and our business development activity be cranked up just to get the business. That is why I predict shorter relationships with clients. True, they may well remember you in their new job, but will it offer the right opportunities? Yes, they may recommend you to the incoming managers, but will they have their own contacts?

Expect tough times ahead and expect to renew clients at an ever faster pace. This means that your ability to get their attention and choose you will be at a premium. So, all those tricks for never making cold calls described earlier in the book (see p. 100) will become ever more necessary as part of your sales armoury.

The arrival of the portfolio consultant

Not only will our clients change, there will be new types of consultant out there too. While some purists might not want to label them out-and-out consultants, my view is that they are, and will have a major impact on the overall business in the years to come. I call them the portfolio consultant. These are bright, intelligent people who have decided that they want to work, but intend to use a variety of skills to provide them with a living.

The first ones I have come across are professionals who took time off for children and now want to work without any commuting hassles or strict time commitments. While they may be a small group at present, I predict that this is a major growth area in the next few years.

Here's an example. The former partner in a highly successful translation business, she took four years off to see her son through his pre-school years. Now that he is headed for school, she wants to work at something interesting, but also be able to take time off when she needs it at holidays and so forth (returning to a nine-to-five job would mean the possibility of just three weeks off each year, certainly to begin with). Using her excellent former client and translator/editor network, she has now set herself up in the following way, using her hard-earned skills:

- *Activity* 1 Freelance editorial consultant. Currently working with two publishers to handle the pre- and post-publication editorial process on specialised books. Organises copy checkers and proof readers, checks texts and recommends changes. Occasional visits to authors and the publishers' offices.
- *Activity* 2 Freelance translator/reviewer. Works with agencies in London, Brussels and Paris revising and reshaping texts. This is fast turnaround activity, but can be carried out anywhere there is a 'space' to download texts.
- *Activity* 3 Freelance research consultant for a leading executive search firm. Following the recession, when all the freelance researchers were forced to

find other work, there is a huge shortage of people. Works on a project-by-project basis that suits her timescale.

- *Activity 4* Bric-a-brac hunter! Her frequent car trips from the UK to Europe are usually underwritten by shipping over 'desirable', cute, bucolic, English 'junk', which Brussels' Eurocrats pay top Euro for.

While never a threat to the top-end independent consultant, people like this are joining the ranks on a daily basis. They are smart, instinctively know how to multitask, and are full of enthusiasm. That's a powerful combination!

Finally: the independent's secret

No book about this noble profession would be complete without a confession (one that I hope other independents will forgive me for): you can do a lot better than most people – on the outside – think.

While I am not suggesting that everyone is going to have the take-home pay equivalent to a senior vice president of a *Fortune 500* corporation, you can make a very comfortable living. And you can do it while making your own decisions and doing business on your own terms.

I recall only too well a younger colleague of mine who quit his job in a large corporation and set up in business on his own. I fed him some work in his early months, and he was a great business developer as well. Sure he worked hard, but he was amazed to discover that after six months he had made a lot more money than he ever had as an employee. Moreover, he had enjoyed himself too! A few of my colleagues and I took him out to lunch to celebrate his discovery that working for yourself could be a lot more lucrative than he had supposed. We left him with the admonition, 'Don't tell anybody.'

Certainly there are times when things go wrong – they do in the big, nasty corporate world as well – but at the end of the day my view is that independent consulting is a lot more fun, and something you can do as long as your brain is working.

Looking back over 20-plus years as an independent I have had a lot of fun, learned a lot and hopefully given good advice and counsel to my clients. But the great thing is that I am not looking at a date on a calendar when I will have to retire. I can do this as long as I want. I may not do quite as much, but it is a better prospect than a sudden end to one's career.

My advice – what this book is for – is to give it a go. You'll never know what it's like until you try. And then, be a pal, DON'T TELL ANYBODY!

Key learning points

- There will be more competitors but also more opportunity as companies seek to outsource and contract out not critical work.
- Technology WILL rule. Like it or not, we shall just have to use it to the best of our abilities.
- We are headed for an era of shorter relationships with clients, brought about by an ever-changing working world. So, expect to spend more time seeking and winning business.
- The portfolio consultant will become the norm, taking on different types of business.
- Finally, 'the secret'. When you discover it's true, don't tell – EVER!

Tax comparison: sole trader v limited company

I N Dependent

TAX COMPARISON – SOLE TRADER V LIMITED COMPANY
TAX YEAR 2005/2006

	Net	Net	VAT rate	VAT	Cash flow
Sales turnover		80,000	17.5%	14,000	94,000
Costs					
Spouse/partners's salary	(4,700)		0.0%	0	(4,700)
Travel	(3,900)		0.0%	0	(3,900)
Accommodation and subsistence	(1,900)		17.5%	(332)	(2,232)
Entertaining	0		0.0%	0	0
Telephone and fax	(1,900)		17.5%	(332)	(2,232)
Motor expenses	(6,000)		17.5%	(1,050)	(7,050)
IT costs	(2,500)		17.5%	(438)	(2,938)
Stationery	(1,000)		17.5%	(175)	(1,175)
Postage	(750)		0.0%	0	(750)
Advertising	(1,500)		17.5%	(263)	(1,763)
Legal and professional fees	(1,200)		0.0%	0	(1,200)
Insurance	(1,100)		0.0%	0	(1,100)
Bank Charges	(1,000)		0.0%	0	(1,000)
Interest on bank loans	(2,550)		0.0%	0	(2,550)
		(30,000)			
Net Profit		50,000			
				11,410	61,410

SUMMARY

	Sole Trader A £	Limited Company Full Salary B £	Limited Company Low Salary with Dividend C £
Net Pay	35,530	28,903	39,494
Total Tax Liability	14,470	15,590	10,506

Key   LL = lower limit   UL = upper limit

A

I N Dependent

TAX ESTIMATE – SOLE TRADER
TAX YEAR 2005/2006

Notes		£	£	Total £
Profit			50,000.00	50,000
Deductions:				
Pension contributions			0.00	
Single Personal allowance			(4,895.00)	
Taxable income			45,105.00	
Tax @ 10%		2,090	209.00	
@ 22%	(Max £30,310)	30,310	6,668.20	
@ 40%		12,705	5,082.00	
		45,105	11,959.20	
			11,959.20	
	(Max £32,760)			
Add: Class 4 NIC @ 8%	(Min £4,895)		2,229.20	
@ 1%	(> £32,760)		172.40	
			14,360.80	
Add: Class 2 NIC (£2.10 pw)			109.20	
			14,470.00	
Total Tax Liability			14,470.00	14,470
Net Pay				35,530

I N Dependent

TAX ESTIMATE – LIMITED COMPANY – FULL SALARY
TAX YEAR 2005/2006

	£		£	£	Total £
Profit				50,000	
Less:					
Salaries (gross)			40,000		
Employers NIC: LL	4,895	12.8%	4,494		4,494
				44,494	
Profit chargeable to Corporation Tax				5,506	
Corporation Tax				0	0
Add:					
Employees NIC: LL	4,895	11%			3,065
Employees NIC: UL	32,760	1%			72
Income tax on salary					7,959
Total Tax Liability					15,591
Salary			40,000		40,000
Less:					
Single personal allowance			(4,895)		
Pension contributions			0		
			35,105		
Tax @ 10%	2,090		209.00		
@ 22%(Max £30,310)	30,310		6,668.20		
@ 40%	2,705		1,082.00		
	35,105		7,959.20		
			7,959.20		
Employee NI			3,137.55		
Personal Tax Due			11,096.75		11,097
Net Pay					28,903
Add: Retained Profit					5,506
					34,409

C

I N Dependent

TAX ESTIMATE – LIMITED COMPANY – LOW SALARY WITH DIVIDENDS
TAX YEAR 2005/2006

	£		£	£	Total £
Profit				50,000	
Less:					
Salaries (gross)			6,000		
Employers NIC: L L	4,895	12.8%	141		141
				6,141	
Profit chargeable to Corporation Tax				43,859	
Corporation Tax				8,278	8,278
Add:					
Employees NIC: LL	4,895	11%			122
Employees NIC: UL	32,760	1%			0
Income tax on salary					111
Income tax on dividend					1,854
Total Tax Liability					10,506
Salary			6,000		6,000
Less:					
Single personal allowance			(4,895)		
Pension contributions			0		
			1,105		
Tax @ 10% (max £2,090)	1,105		110.50		
@ 22% (max £30,310)	0		0.00		
@ 40%	0		0.00		
	1,105		110.50		
Employee NI			121.55		
Personal Tax Due			232.05		(232)

	Gross	Tax (£)	Net	
Add: Dividend	39,534	3,953	35,580	35,580
Less: Higher rate tax liability			1,854	(1,854)
			33,727	
Net Pay				39,494
Add: Retained Profit				0
				34,494

Appendix 2

IR35 – A quick guide

Are you caught by the IR 35 PSC Rules or not?

There are 5 key status tests:

1. No mutuality of obligation ('MOO')

2. Are you in business on your own account?

3. Fundamental status tests:
   - Substitution.
   - Significant financial risk assumed by you (and the ability for you to profit from sound management).
   - Do you have the ability to hire others to do the work (intrinsic to the engagement – not just secretarial and admin. support)?

4. Important status tests:
   - Provision of significant equipment.
   - Who has control over what you do?
   - The length and number of different assignments/engagements each year.

5. Minor status tests:
   - Exclusivity.
   - Terms of payment.
   - Rights of dismissal.
   - The intentions of you and the contractor for whom you work as to how the arrangement should operate.
   - Business structure.

What happens if you are caught by the anti-avoidance legislation?

All of the fees from any assignment that is caught are effectively subject to PAYE tax and National Insurance contributions (both employer and employee contributions) except that the following deductions can be made:

1. 5% of the gross income to cover admin and running costs.

2 Travel, accommodation and subsistence:

   i Travel costs *excluding*:
  - Private travel
  - Ordinary commuting

     But including travel to temporary workplace.
(Workplace is temporary if either: less than 40% of the duties of the employment carried out there at this workplace *or* the engagement is expected to last for less than two years.)

   ii Motor costs based on the Inland Revenue AMR scale rates (effectively 40p per mile per business trip for the first 10,000 miles and 25p per mile thereafter) for *business* mileage (but see (i) for what is allowable).

   iii Accommodation and subsistence, if appropriate.

3 Professional indemnity insurance.

4 Capital allowances on equipment used for the business.

5 Employer's pension contributions.

6 Salary and PAYE and NIC already paid on payroll salaries.

Example

An example of how this 'deemed payment' calculation would look is as follows:

Mr Bloggs works for his own limited company (Bloggs Limited) and provides services to Client Plc under a contract which falls within the IR35 rules. Bloggs Limited receives £40,000 per annum for the service supplied to Client Plc. Bloggs Limited pays Mr Bloggs an annual salary of £10,000 and PAYE and National Insurance is operated thereon. Employer's National Insurance of £672 is paid annually by Bloggs Limited on that salary. The company also provides Mr Bloggs with a company car and the taxable benefit in kind value thereon is £2,000 and Class 1A NIC thereon is £256.

   Bloggs Limited's other expenses are:

	£
Motor running expenses (MRE) (50% use business)	3,000
Pension contributions	1,200
Training costs	500
(Training not imposed by client plc)	
Professional subscriptions	450
Professional indemnity insurance (PII)	500
Employer and public liability insurance	400
Capital allowances/depreciation (Equipment)	1,000
Capital allowances/depreciation (Car)	500
Accountancy fees	500
	8,050

	£
Step 1	
Income received	40,000
Less: 5% allowance	(2,000)
Step 2	
Allowable expenses	
MRE (50%)	(1,500)
Professional subscriptions	(450)
PII	(500)
Step 3	
Capital allowances	
Equipment	(1,000)
Step 4	
Pension contributions	(1,200)
Step 5	
Employers NIC (Class 1 and 1A)	(928)
Step 6	
Salary and benefits	(12,000)
Balance	20,422
GROSS deemed payment (20,422/1.128)	(18,104)
Employer's National Insurance payable	2,318

PAYE and National Insurance deemed payment is due on or by 19 April each year after the tax year ends on 5 April.

Corporation Tax

Based on the same example above, the profit and loss account would be as follows:

	£	£
Turnover		40,000
Less: Overheads		
Salary	10,000	
Deemed payment	18,104	
Employer's NI on salary and benefits	928	
Employer's NI on deemed payment	2,318	
Motor running expenses (MRE)	3,000	
Pension contributions	1,200	
Training costs	500	
Professional subscriptions	450	
Professional indemnity insurance (PII)	500	
Employer and public liability insurance	400	
Depreciation	1,500	
Accountancy fees	500	
		(39,400)
Net profit		600

And, assuming no dividend paid and no other associated companies, then the corporation tax payable is Nil as the net profit is within the nil rate band of £10,000

Year end

If you are caught by the IR35 PSC rules, you should ideally have a '5 April' year end for your company accounts. This will facilitate the calculation of the deemed payment and of any PAYE and National Insurance thereon.

Note that the items reflected in the deemed payment calculation are purely on a receipts and payments basis. Hence debtors and creditors should be excluded.

Protecting yourself

- Have your contract vetted (and approved) first by the Inland Revenue.
- Have your contract vetted by specialist insurers who, if they confirm that your company is not an IR35 company, would be prepared to underwrite at a premium any subsequent tax and National Insurance charge.

- If your contract is approved by an IR35 specialist recognized by insurers such as Abbey Tax, take out insurance to cover extra tax and national insurance that may be payable if the Inland Revenue later deems your company to be covered by IR35 legislation. The premium costs around £500–600 p.a.
- Take out insurance to cover the costs of an Inland Revenue enquiry (this does *not* cover the cost of any extra tax or NIC that may be payable). This is a cheaper option to the one above.

Extracting funds from your PSC

The most tax effective means of extracting funds from your PSC would be to claim most expenses allowable under IR35 regulations and, after allowing for the 5 per cent allowance, to draw the balance of the company's income as salary.

As a deemed payment will attract PAYE and National Insurance, it would be advisable for your company to pay you a gross bonus of an amount equivalent to the gross deemed payment before 19 April in order for you to enjoy the cash.

Another way to extract funds would be to vote a dividend equivalent to the deemed payment and, provided PAYE and National Insurance has been paid on the deemed payment, to obtain clearance from the Inland Revenue dealing with your company's tax affairs so that the dividend is not taxed twice.

What happens if you are not caught by the anti-avoidance legislation?

Carry on regardless – you are lucky!

Think what you will save in accountancy fees …

Appendix 3

Sample consultancy agreement

BETWEEN: **Name here** (Hereinafter referred as the Company)

AND: **Name here** (Hereinafter referred to as the Consultant)

WHEREAS:

Whereas the Company wishes to obtain advisory and consulting services from the Consultant as its independent external consultant for business development and the Consultant agrees to assist the Company with such services as an independent external consultant under the terms and the conditions set forth in this Agreement.

NOW THEREFORE IT HAS BEEN AGREED AS FOLLOWS:

Article 1 Subject

1 The Company hereby appoints the Consultant as its external consultant and the Consultant hereby agrees to provide independent advisory and consulting services to the Company in the field of (to be completed).

2 The tasks of the Consultant shall consist in the development of new clients (approved in advance by the Company) in the aforestated field including discussion of terms and conditions with actual or potential clients but with the exception of the signing of any contractual undertaking in that respect, unless specifically authorised by the Company.

3 The Consultant shall carry out its services as specified in the present Consultancy Agreement.

Article 2 Duration and termination

1 This contract (hereafter the Agreement) shall enter into force for an indefinite duration on (to be completed).

2 The present Agreement may be terminated by each party with one (1) month advance written notice per commenced period of seniority of one (1) year and without exceeding in total six (6) months sent by registered mail, which takes effect the third working day following the date of mailing. The end of the notice coinciding with the end of the calendar month.

3 In the event that the serious misconduct or serious fault is of such a nature that it renders impossible the definitive continuation of any professional relationship, the aggrieved party shall have the right to terminate the Consultancy

Agreement at once, without notice or indemnity, by sending a registered letter to the other party in which the termination is effected and by sending, also by registered mail, within seven (7) days thereof the facts or reason justifying such termination for cause.

4 The Agreement shall automatically terminate in case of death or disability of the Consultant without notice or indemnity.

Article 3 Conditions of performance of services

1 The Consultant shall perform the services in a completely independent manner and under its sole responsibility. The Consultant cannot commit or otherwise bind the Company unless specifically authorised by the Company. The services provided under this contract shall be rendered by the Consultant, via its President or via any other person designated by the Consultant subject to the prior express approval of the Company.

2 The Consultant shall perform the services conscientiously and shall devote his best efforts and abilities thereto, at such time during the term thereof, in such manner as the Company and the Consultant shall mutually agree.

3 The Consultant shall perform his activities under the present Agreement on an entirely independent basis and will never act or consider himself as an employee or agent of the Company. This agreement shall not constitute a partnership between the parties hereto.

Without prejudice to its general obligation of proper performance of the services, the Consultant shall be able, with complete freedom and independence, to organise its activities and shall only have to render account of the specific duties or services accomplished under the present Agreement, but shall not be required to account for his working methods. The Company shall never exert over the Consultant any part of authority, which an employer is normally vested with.

The Consultant is solely responsible for the payment of the social security contributions and tax obligations, including VAT, with respect to the fees paid under the present Agreement.

4 This Consultancy Agreement is non-exclusive. The Company is free to consult other experts in the Consultant's field of specialisation and the Consultant retains the right to provide similar services to other parties, unless those parties carry on any activities in competition with the activities of the Company.

Article 4 Copyright/Confidentiality

1 The Consultant transfers to the Company, the future copyright in or on any and all written documents prepared by the Consultant for the Company or upon the Company's request within the framework of this Agreement.

2 The Consultant acknowledges that during the course of the consulting activities within the framework of this Agreement confidential information regarding the Company may be exchanged between the contracting parties. The Consultant shall keep secret and confidential all such information during the course of the Agreement and after the termination of this Agreement. The Consultant shall not use such information other than for this Agreement.

Such information includes but is not limited to:
- all drawings, formulae, specifications, books, software, instruction manuals, daily reports, minutes of meetings, journals and accounts, business and trade secrets, oral or written data, whether concerning the existing or future business, methods, processes, techniques or equipment of the Company, its parent Company, subsidiaries or branch offices
- the identity of the clients Company, its parent company, subsidiaries or branch offices and any other information relating to such clients.

3 Any violation of the secrecy obligation during the course of the present Agreement may be considered by the Company as a cause justifying immediate termination of the present Agreement, without notice and without prejudice to the right of the Company to claim damages.

4 Upon termination of this Agreement or upon the Company's request, the Consultant shall return to the Company all documents of whatever nature, notes, reports, letters and faxes relating to the Company and which he has received for the execution of the present Agreement.

Article 5 Non-competition and unfair competition
The Consultant will refrain from actively soliciting the clients for which he has actively worked during the last two years under this Agreement for a period of one (1) year after termination of this Agreement, in areas associated with this agreement.

Article 6 Compensation
1 In the event that the Consultant brings in an assignment, the Company shall pay (after receiving payment from the client) a fee equal to 10% (10 per cent) in the first year, 7.5% (7.5 per cent) in the second year and 5% (5 per cent) in the third year of the monthly net sum billed to the clients brought by the Consultant, during a period of three years following the first invoice sent to the client by the Company. The consultant shall be paid in (*state currency*).

When the Consultant is working for the Company, on their request, on projects gained by the Company, the Company shall pay to the Consultant a fixed daily fee in (*state currency plus VAT*). This fee shall be determined in advance by the Company and paid against submission of a monthly invoice.

2 The Consultant has the right to ask documents relating to the amounts billed to the clients and the payments made by clients in order to verify the amount due to him.

3 In addition to the compensation fixed in the first paragraph of this article, subject to the remittance of invoices, notes or any mutually acceptable evidence, the Company shall also reimburse expenses, subject to prior approval by the Company.

In case there exists already contacts with the client and the Company, no fees will be due to the Consultant, unless the development of that relationship with the client is approved in advance in writing by the Company.

4 Upon termination of this Agreement, for whatever reason, the Consultant shall be entitled to receive the contractual compensation for all business brought until the date of actual termination of the agreement.

Except in case of termination for cause, the Consultant shall also be entitled to the contractual compensation for any business brought by him or attributable to him, which the Company can invoice to such clients within six (6) months following the date of actual termination of the Agreement.

Article 7 Assignment
No party to this Agreement may assign or delegate any of its/his right, duties, powers or responsibilities thereunder without prior consent of the other party, given in writing.

Article 8 Notice
All notices to be given under this Agreement, except in case of termination, shall be made by registered mail or by courier to the address of each party.

Article 9 Severance and public restrictions
If any provision of this Agreement is declared void or unenforceable by any judicial or administrative authority, this shall not nullify the remaining provisions of this Agreement, provided that the cancellation of such provision does not substantially alter the economic interest of either party in the continued performance of this Agreement.

Article 10 Governing law and Jurisdiction
This Agreement is governed and interpreted in accordance with the laws of (*state country or State*). Any dispute arising in connection with this Agreement and which cannot be settled on an amicable basis shall be submitted to the exclusive jurisdiction of Courts of such State.

Article 11 Prior agreements
This Agreement constitutes the entire agreement between the parties relative to

the matters referred to herein and supersedes any other agreement, whether oral or writing, which may have existed between the Company and the Consultant.

Any modification or amendments of this Agreement shall be in writing and shall become effective if and when signed by both parties.

Executed in two (2) original copies, each party acknowledging having receipt of one original copy,

By: _____   _____

Date

By: _____   _____

Date

Appendix 4

Websites and information sources

Accountants	www.icaew.co.uk
	www.accaglobal.com
	www.cima.org.uk
	www.cta.org.uk
Solicitors	www.lawsociety.org.uk
Banks	www.barclays.co.uk
	www.hsbc.co.uk
	www.lloydstsb.com
	www.natwest.com
	www.find.co.uk
Bookkeeping and accounts packages	www.sage.com
	www.access-accounts.com
	www.simplybooks.net
	www.iris.co.uk
	www.myob.co.uk
	www.quickbooks.co.uk
Business link	www.businesslink.gov.uk
Government	www.dti.gov.uk
Income tax and national insurance	www.hmrc.gov.uk
Small firms loan guarantee scheme	www.businesslink.gov.uk
Professional contractors	www.pcg.org.uk
	www.hmrc.gov.uk
	www.ir35calc.co.uk
Tax	See Income Tax and VAT
VAT	www.hmrc.gov.uk

Index

The Coach's Coach

Personal development for personal developers

Alison Hardingham
with Mike Brearley, Adrian Moorhouse and Brendan Venter

Being a coach is a tricky job, so whether you are an experienced coach or just starting out; a specialist consultant or a coaching manager, this book will help you become better and enjoy coaching more. It will help you to help the people you are coaching improve their performance – which, after all, is why you became a coach in the first place.

Alison Hardingham is a successful business coach and offers advice, techniques and examples drawn from experience of coaching people in all kinds of organisations and with the contributions of three phenomenally successful sports people: Mike Brearley, Adrian Moorhouse and Brendan Venter, you will be on track to being 'coach of the year'.

Mike Brearly is one of England's best known and most successful cricket captain; **Adrian Moorhouse** broke the world record in breast stroke five times and won an Olympic gold medal; and **Brendan Venter** was a member of the Springboks, South African Rugby Team, and subsequently played and coached at London Irish.

Order your copy now by visiting us online at www.cipd.co.uk/bookstore or call us on 0870 800 3366

Alison Hardingham is a business psychologist with more than twenty years' experience of coaching individuals and teams. She is a successful author and conference speaker.

2004	1 84398 075 4	Paperback	216 pages

The Chartered Institute of Personnel and Development is the leading publisher of books and reports for personnel and training professionals, students, and for all those concerned with the effective management and development of people at work.

Also from CIPD Publishing . . .

The New Rules of Engagement:

Life–work balance and employee commitment

Mike Johnson

How many of your employees care enough about their work, or organisation, to do anything more than the bare minimum? How many would stay if they were offered another job?

Highly-engaged employees are six times less likely to be planning to leave their employer than the disengaged. How much could you save on recruitment costs by improving engagement? How about the 'discretionary effort' that highly engaged employees put in?

This text argues that there are ways to develop a new psychological contract between employer and employee. Start by recognising that talk of a 'work–life balance' is the wrong way round as far as employees are concerned – they are much more interested in a 'life–work balance'.

The advice in this book will:
- help to convince senior management that employee engagement matters;
- help to improve your employees' productivity and willingness to try out new ideas and work practices;
- help to retain key employees; and
- make it easier to attract a higher calibre of employee.

Order your copy now online at www.cipd.co.uk/bookstore or call us on 0870 800 3366

Mike Johnson is a consultant, author and Managing Partner of Johnson Associates Limited, a coprorate communications consultancy. The firm's main activities are internal communications strategy, researching and writing on world-of-work issues, and management education strategy for major corporations and institutions.

Published 2004	1 84398 072 X	Paperback	192 pages

The Chartered Institute of Personnel and Development is the leading publisher of books and reports for personnel and training professionals, students and all those concerned with the effective management and development of people at work.